CO-ACR-120

GUIDE TO
SELLING YOUR
HOME

ATHENS REGIONAL LIBRARY
2025 BAXTER STREET
ATHENS, GA 30606

Real Estate
Education Company®
a division of Dearborn Financial Publishing, Inc.

This publication is designed to provide accurate and authoritative information in regard to the subject matter covered. It is sold with the understanding that the publisher is not engaged in rendering legal, accounting or other professional service. If legal advice or other expert assistance is required, the services of a competent professional person should be sought.

Acquisitions Editor: Christine E. Litavsky
Managing Editor: Jack Kiburz
Project Editor: Karen Christensen
Cover Design: ST & Associates
Interior Design: Lucy Jenkins
Typesetting: Elizabeth Pitts

© 1997 by Dearborn Financial Publishing, Inc.®

Published by Real Estate Education Company®,
a division of Dearborn Financial Publishing, Inc.®

All rights reserved. The text of this publication, or any part thereof, may not be reproduced in any manner whatsoever without written permission from the publisher.

Printed in the United States of America

97 98 99 10 9 8 7 6 5 4 3 2 1

Library of Congress Cataloging-in-Publication Data

CENTURY 21® guide to selling your home : 50 insider secrets for a top
   dollar sale / CENTURY 21®.
     p. cm.
   Includes index.
   ISBN 0-7931-2295-3
   1. House selling—Handbooks, manuals, etc.   I. CENTURY 21®.
HD1379.C454   1997
333.33′83—dc20   96-9858
                                   CIP

Real Estate Education Company books are available at special quantity discounts to use as premiums and sales promotions, or for use in corporate training programs. For more information, please call the Special Sales Manager at 800-621-9621, ext. 4384, or write to Dearborn Financial Publishing, Inc., 155 N. Wacker Drive, Chicago, IL 60606-1719.

Find This Book Useful for Your Real Estate Needs?

Discover all the bestselling CENTURY 21® Guides:

CENTURY 21® Guide to Buying Your Home

CENTURY 21® Guide to Choosing Your Mortgage

CENTURY 21® Guide to Inspecting Your Home

CENTURY 21® Guide to Selling Your Home

CONTENTS

PREFACE

Selling your home can be a bewildering and frustrating experience. But if you know what to expect and what all your options are before you sell, the experience can be exciting and rewarding. The *CENTURY 21® Guide to Selling Your Home* provides the background information and expert advice you need to sell your house for the best price and with the least amount of effort. You'll learn how to get the house ready for sale, how to price and market the house, what to do if the house doesn't sell and more.

Step-by-step, this information-packed book leads you through the process of selling your home—from making the decision to sell and picking the right agent, through the tax effects after the sale.

This book is packed with 50 money-saving tips collected from our top professionals and is designed to help you preserve the dollars you need to pursue your next homebuying adventure. To address lingering doubts or concerns, each chapter ends with answers to the questions most commonly asked by homeowners like you.

It's what you'd expect from the company that symbolizes home ownership—and whose brokers and associates in your community stand at the ready to help you put these strategies into action.

All of us in the *CENTURY* 21® System—*the* source for homeowner information and services—wish you the best in your house selling venture, and many years of happy living.

CHAPTER 1

Deciding to Sell Your Home

Unless you're the rare exception, you will move several times during your lifetime. In fact, surveys by the National Association of REALTORS® and other organizations indicate that the average American household moves once every seven years. Here are some of the reasons why:

Common Reasons for Moving

- Need more space to accommodate a growing family
- Need less space—these people are often *empty nesters* (parents whose children have left home) who want to downsize to a smaller house
- Need to relocate because of a new job or to be closer to current job
- Desire better location (present house may be in a declining neighborhood)
- Divorce or death of a spouse forces sale of house

- Owner can no longer afford the house
- Owner wants to move up to a bigger or better house
- Owner wants to retire and move elsewhere
- No particular reason—simply want a change

Why Do You Want to Sell?

Before you decide to sell your home, you should take a careful look at *why* you want to move. It's easy to put your home on the market for the wrong reason. If you have to move because of your job, you may have no choice in the matter. If you are moving simply because you want to live in a different house, that may not be a good enough reason—especially when the costs far outweigh the benefits.

Move or Improve?

When your motivation for selling is the need for more living space, you must decide whether to add on to your present home or buy another. If you love the location of your home, adding new space or making old space work better may be cheaper and less disruptive than moving. Take a hard look at the house you live in and assess its problems realistically. You may decide to adopt the "Don't move, improve" philosophy and remodel your old home instead of building or buying a new one.

Keep in mind, however, that remodeling a house is not always worth the investment—particularly if the home already compares with better-than-average homes in the area. You don't want to price yourself out of the resale market. As a general rule of thumb, appraisers, mortgage lenders and others have found that, no matter how much you improve any given house, you're unlikely to sell it for more than 15 percent above the median price of other houses in the neighborhood.

On the other hand, if the house can't be redone to suit your needs, you'll know you really do want to move.

Create a List

Before you decide to pack up and move, it would probably be a good idea to analyze what you like and dislike about your present home. You'll also have a better understanding of what to look for in your next home.

A good way to start is by making a list of all the things you don't like about your house. Note whether you can change any of the dislikes into likes. For example, if you could change your house, what would be different? Would you have central air? More bedrooms? A fireplace? You can make these kinds of changes. Some changes are impossible to make, however. If you want a bigger lot, a better view or a more desirable location, you'll need to find a new house.

Next, make a list of what you do like about your house. Perhaps you like the neighborhood and its accessibility to schools, shops and transportation. Maybe the house has a backyard with a wood deck and other outdoor amenities that you enjoy. You may find that you like your house more than you realize and are willing to consider alternatives to moving. In any case, listing your likes and dislikes will help you recognize exactly what you want in your next home.

Take a few minutes to create your own list of likes and dislikes. You can use the blank form in Figure 1.1.

Now think about exactly what you want in your new house. Figure 1.2 is a checklist of things you should consider. Space is provided at the end of the list so you can enter additional features of interest to you.

☞ **Money-$aving Tip #1** *Moving can be costly. So when you consider your replacement home, think about how your needs and wants may change in the years ahead.*

FIGURE 1.1 Likes and Dislikes

Things I Don't Like about My House	Things I Do Like about My House
1. _____	_____
2. _____	_____
3. _____	_____
4. _____	_____
5. _____	_____
6. _____	_____
7. _____	_____
8. _____	_____
9. _____	_____
10. _____	_____
11. _____	_____
12. _____	_____
13. _____	_____
14. _____	_____
15. _____	_____

☞ **Money-$aving Tip #2** *If you think you may have to resell again soon, buy a replacement home with features that will appeal to the majority of prospective buyers.*

Timing the Sale

When is the best time to sell your house? As soon as you decide to sell it. Only you can determine how ready you are to move. And when you are ready to move, you are ready to sell.

FIGURE 1.2 Key Features Checklist

❑ Price range: _____ - _____   **Garage**

❑ Square feet: _____   ❑ One-car

❑ Number of bedrooms: _____   ❑ Two-car

❑ Number of bathrooms: _____   ❑ Carport

Living Area   **Other Amenities**

❑ Master suite   ❑ Storage room

❑ Fireplace   ❑ Laundry room

❑ Central air-conditioning   ❑ Wood deck

❑ A room that can be turned   ❑ Patio
   into an office
                                      ❑ Swimming pool

❑ Den   ❑ View

❑ Living room   ❑ _____

❑ Family room   ❑ _____

❑ Formal dining room   ❑ _____

❑ L-shaped dining area   ❑ _____

Kitchen Layout   ❑ _____

❑ Single-counter   ❑ _____

❑ L-shaped   ❑ _____

❑ U-shaped   ❑ _____

❑ Island

Traditionally, late spring and early summer have been the peak home selling seasons. Families with school-aged children usually prefer to make their buying decisions in time to be settled in their new home before school begins in the fall.

The weather also has a lot to do with establishing peak selling seasons. For example, late spring and early fall are the peak selling seasons in many areas because houses tend to "show" better in those months than they do in the heat of summer or the cold of winter. That is, flowers in bloom, healthy green grass and colorful leaves on trees help create a more pleasing setting for a house than do bare trees, dried-up grass and dirty, slushy snow. Also, people like to do their house hunting in pleasant, more comfortable weather.

But keep in mind that there are also more homes on the market during the peak selling seasons, increasing the level of competition. So while there is seasonality in the housing market, it shouldn't dominate your decision on when to sell.

What Costs Are Involved?

Selling a house in today's real estate market is more difficult than it has been in years, and more costs are involved than you may realize.

Repair expenses. These are typically cosmetic repairs that will improve your chances for making a sale; for example, painting the front door and trim around the house, improving the landscaping, fixing cracks in the driveway, repapering a faded wall in the master bedroom, replacing a worn-out carpet—all the things that must be done to get the home in "show" condition.

Sales commission. You are responsible for the fee charged by your real estate agent. Such fees are entirely negotiable.

Closing costs. The seller's closing costs will vary depending on local custom, the lender involved and what you have agreed to in the sales contract. No hard-and-fast rules apply. The closing process will be covered in a later chapter.

Moving expenses. These include the costs of hiring a moving company or renting a moving truck if you plan to do it yourself.

Costs of buying a house. In addition to the down payment, you, as the buyer, will have to pay costs connected with the mortgage loan, such as a credit check fee, a loan application fee and a loan origination fee.

☞ **Money-$aving Tip #3** *Many costs are involved in selling a house. If you love the location of your home but simply need more room, it may be financially more prudent to add on than to move.*

Seller's Market versus Buyer's Market

A market is simply a means for bringing buyers and sellers together. Depending on the economy, you may find yourself in a *seller's market* (many more buyers than sellers) or a *buyer's market* (many more sellers than buyers).

During most of the 1980s, the country experienced a seller's market for homes. This meant that sellers had the stronger negotiating position. Sellers knew that if they didn't get their asking price, all they had to do was wait and the value of their homes would increase. But those days are long gone. They ended in 1987 with the stock market crash, the savings-and-loan crisis and the start of a lengthy recession.

If you are selling one home and buying another, as many people do, it really doesn't make much difference what kind of market (buyer or seller) exists because you will have an advantage at one end or the other. For example, if you sell in a buyer's market, you'll most likely also have to buy in the same kind of market. So you really don't lose or gain anything.

How *Your Agent Can Help*

Whatever your motivation for moving, professional real estate brokers or agents can assist you in many ways. For example, they can help determine if selling is your best option; help you sell one home and look for another at the same time; and even assist you in making the move.

If you have an eye toward adding on instead of moving, it's important to determine what structural and code limitations you may have. Ask for your agent's opinion on your home's potential for enlargement and for information about setbacks and other zoning restrictions that might limit the kinds of changes you could make. Any information your agent does not know can be gleaned by calls to inspectors, builders, structural engineers, architects and other specialists.

If you're selling one home and buying another, your agent can

- help you determine exactly what you need in a new home;
- help you select houses to tour;
- make appointments to see those homes;
- transport you to the homes you're touring;
- help you evaluate those homes;
- help you estimate the value of homes you are interested in purchasing; and more.

☞ **Money-$aving Tip #4** *Be cautious of buying a second home before you sell the one you live in, especially in a slow real estate market. Unless you're rich, owning two houses in a buyer's market can be financially disastrous.*

Commonly Asked Questions

Q. *Should I put my home on the market first or wait until I find the one I want to buy?*

A. Most people put their house on the market first and then start looking for a new house at about the same time. Keep in mind, however, that if you buy your new home before you sell your existing one, you run the risk of being stuck with two mortgages for a while. This possibility may pressure you into accepting an offer on your existing house that you wouldn't even consider under normal circumstances. On the other hand, if you sell your existing house first, you'll have a better idea of your financial picture when it comes time to buy your new home. Under this scenario, of course, there is the possibility that you'll end up having to make temporary living arrangements until you buy your new house.

Q. *Suppose I find my next house before I sell my current one. How can I avoid ending up with two houses and two mortgages?*

A. You can make the purchase of your new house contingent on the sale of your existing house. Obviously, sellers are not fond of this type of contingency because it ties up their property with no guarantees. A likely alternative for sellers is to limit your contingency by keeping their house on the market and giving you the right of first refusal if another offer is received.

Q. *Should market conditions have any bearing on when I list?*

A. Probably not. A house can be sold at the right price in any real estate market with an effective marketing plan.

Q. What does it mean to overimprove my house?

A. Overimprovement means making changes to the house, such as adding a room, that cost more than the increased value of the house; that is, putting more money into the house than neighborhood prices will support.

Q. How do you know when you're overimproving?

A. When remodeling an existing house, homeowners run the risk of overimproving their property to the point of not being able to recover their costs when it comes time to sell. But how do you know when you're overdoing it? How much improvement is too much? The neighborhood is the key. Bring the house up to what's the standard around the neighborhood, but don't exceed the uppermost limit—otherwise, you're likely not to recover your costs.

A house that has been overimproved usually stands out from the others on the block. It is the house with the oak-and-leaded-glass front door next to the ones with simple, painted doors. The overimproved house has the only pool and Jacuzzi in the neighborhood. Or it has four bedrooms in a predominantly two-bedroom community.

When a For Sale sign goes up on the front lawn of a house that has been overimproved, it's usually there for quite some time—until the owner lowers the price or the owner finds a buyer who thinks the add-ons justify the price.

Q. Should I add on to my present home or buy another one?

A. It may be less costly and certainly less disruptive to stay put if

- you like your neighborhood;
- your reason for moving is the need for more living space; and
- it's feasible to expand without overimproving.

```
┌─────────────────────────┐
│  ┌───────────────────┐  │
│  │   C H A P T E R  2 │  │
│  └───────────────────┘  │
└─────────────────────────┘
```

Agent versus FSBO (For Sale by Owner)

Selling a home involves much more than just placing an ad in a newspaper or magazine and then taking calls from prospective buyers. You have to set the asking price, market the house, negotiate offers, qualify buyers, handle the closing and more. This chapter will help you decide whether to use an agent or try to sell the home yourself.

Agent or FSBO?

The primary motivation in selling a home yourself is to save the commission that would have to be paid to an agent. But selling real estate is hard work. There's a lot of rejection to deal with and long, long hours. You'll have to put up with the hassles of screening prospective buyers; stay home so you can escort them from room to room; worry about whether they're qualified to get a mortgage; and deal with the many details that arise in every house sale from the first showing through the closing.

If you are toying with the idea of selling your house yourself, first consider what an agent can do for you. After reviewing this information, you should be able to decide whether it's worth the time and effort to go it alone.

What the Agent Does

An agent offers many services that will facilitate the sale of your home. He or she will help you with the following:

- *Recommend an asking price for your home, based on recent listing and selling prices of comparable houses in your neighborhood.* Of course, you want the most money you can get from your home, but you must be objective and realistic about the asking price you set. A home that is overpriced is not going to sell. Setting a realistic price is the first step toward a successful sale.
- *Give advice on repairs and renovations.* An agent can look at your home objectively and tell you what changes are needed to make your house more appealing to buyers. Often, all that's necessary may be cleaning, painting and minor repairs.
- *Advertise in your local newspaper.* Today's brokers, especially larger ones, use a variety of other proven advertising methods, including magazines, TV, direct mail and the Internet.
- *Screen house-hunters to determine whether they are financially capable of buying your home.*
- *Market your house through the Multiple Listing Service (MLS), a computerized collection of all listed homes.* This service dramatically increases the exposure of your home to a large number of potential buyers.
- *Handle all appointments to show the house.*

- *Conduct open-house tours for prospective buyers and other agents.*
- *Give you timely progress reports.* It's important for you to know what's going on, how many prospective buyers have seen your home and what the response has been—negative as well as positive.
- *Present all offers in writing.*
- *Handle negotiations with the buyer.* There's a lot of give and take when a real estate deal is being negotiated. A good real estate agent is a skilled negotiator who creates a win-win situation, one in which all parties are satisfied with the process and the outcome.
- *Help a buyer find appropriate financing.*
- *Oversee the closing process.* An agent makes sure all the details are taken care of so that the closing can proceed smoothly. These include making arrangements for title evidence, surveys, appraisals, inspections or repairs and more. In addition, you'll find your agent to be a valuable source of advice and counsel at the closing itself.

☞ **Money-$aving Tip #5** *A real estate agent has an enormous amount of information at his or her disposal that can help make your home sell faster. That translates into savings for you.*

Do You Still Want to Sell on Your Own?

Now that you know what an agent does, you may still want to try selling your home yourself. Keep in mind, however, that a high percentage of FSBO (agents call them "Fizzbos") attempts fail and the homeowners eventually end up working with real estate agents. That doesn't mean you shouldn't give it a shot. It just means you should be prepared for the difficulties involved in selling your home on your own.

☞ **Money-$aving Tip #6** *If you're going to go the FSBO route, put in a lot of time and effort when the house is fresh on the market—the first 30 days or so. This is the best time to make a sale. Then, if things don't work out during this period, consider listing the house with a broker.*

Today, about 20 percent of homeowners handle their own sales. But in order to be successful, you need to assess exactly what's involved in the selling process. You need to price your home realistically, determine whether a prospective buyer is qualified, create and pay for your own advertising, familiarize yourself with enough basic real estate regulations to understand a sales contract, coordinate the details of a closing and more.

The biggest negatives about selling on your own are the demand on your time and the possibility that a mistake may cost you the money you're trying to save.

Another negative point about selling your home on your own is that you won't have access to your local Multiple Listing Service, so your house won't get the exposure an MLS can provide. That can be a substantial drawback, especially in a slow market.

Finally, you'll have to spend some of your own money for advertising and other marketing expenses. This could cost you a few bucks if the house doesn't sell quickly.

Despite the difficulties, many people do sell their own homes. The ones most likely to succeed study the market carefully, prepare their properties and use lawyers, brokers and agents as consultants paid on an hourly basis.

☞ **Money-$aving Tip #7** *The best time to be a FSBO is in a hot market, when homes in the area are selling quickly. Self-selling is not a good choice when the market is slow. There are fewer buyers in a slow market, so the worth and importance of broker or agent services are likely to increase.*

How *Your Agent Can Help*

Most homeowners are not willing to put in the time and effort it takes to sell a house. And most lack the real estate knowledge, experience and data needed to sell their homes successfully. That's why most sellers choose to take advantage of the services provided by a real estate agent—a licensed professional who earns a living by bringing buyers and sellers together and is paid only when the sale is completed.

Real estate agents have a tremendous amount of information at their disposal—information that can help make your home sell faster, easier and at the right price. They know about market trends, houses in your neighborhood and the kinds of people most likely to buy there. They also know how to reach the largest number of people who may be interested in your home. Real estate agents are trained in such areas as pricing, marketing and showing your home. They screen potential buyers, negotiate with them and give advice on the pros and cons of each offer. Real estate agents offer financing hints and suggestions to your buyer, participate in the closing, and do all the things it takes to make a deal work. And they are always "on call." They work on weekends, answer the phone at all hours and are always available to answer any questions prospective buyers may have. In short, your real estate agent has the expertise to go along with the time, money and effort it takes to sell your home reasonably quickly and at a good price.

☞ **Money-$aving Tip #8** *If you're selling on your own and an agent drops by with an interested buyer, ask whether the agent will accept a reduced commission.*

Commonly Asked Questions

Q. *What makes a home sell?*

A. There are five basic things to consider: the price, the terms, the condition, the location and the exposure.

Q. *If I am self-selling my home, can I list it in the MLS?*

A. No. Only MLS members can list homes in the Multiple Listing Service, the computer database that informs other agents and prospective buyers that your home is for sale.

Q. *Should I list with a brokerage who doesn't belong to the local MLS?*

A. Probably not—unless they can give you a good reason why they don't belong. Such a brokerage won't have access to as many of the serious buyers in your area as will a brokerage that does belong to the MLS. In many areas, the MLS is the entry point for eight out of ten sales.

Q. *Is an agent more likely to find a buyer than I am on my own?*

A. Yes, especially in a slow market—unless, however, you are incredibly lucky. An agent can draw immediately from his or her own pool of qualified prospective buyers, some of whom are probably looking for homes like yours. And, if your house is listed in your local MLS—as it should be—numerous other agents with their own potential buyers will have the chance to sell it.

CHAPTER 3

Picking the Right Agent

Selling a home is a complex matter involving pricing, marketing, financing and a lot of administrative details. Choosing the right real estate agent is often the first step in selling a house successfully. But finding that agent can be an exercise in frustration and uncertainty. More than a few sellers end up asking, "How do I know if this agent is the one for me?" The answer, of course, is there is no foolproof method for picking an agent. And to make things worse, the real estate market has become increasingly crowded and competitive in the past few years.

The true test of an agent's competence, of course, is performance. Is the agent going to go out there and market your home, protect your interests and get the best possible deal for you? The catch is that you can't really know how an agent will perform until a listing has been signed and the agent is actually out there working for you. But if the agent has a good track record, chances are pretty good that he or she will perform well for you.

The Basics

All real estate agents are required to be licensed by the state in which they sell. Licensees fall into three categories:

1. Brokers
2. Associate brokers
3. Agents or salespeople

All states require that prospective licensees pass an objective, written examination. Almost all require formal classroom training.

A broker is authorized to operate his or her own real estate business and is responsible for the entire operation; anyone licensed with a broker can operate only in the name of and under the supervision of that broker. An associate broker is someone who has qualified as a real estate broker but still works for and is supervised by the broker in charge. The agent/salesperson—with whom you have most of your day-to-day contact—also works on behalf of, and is compensated by, the broker.

The REALTOR®

REALTOR® is a registered trademark of the *National Association of REALTORS®* (NAR), the largest and best-known real estate organization in the world. The NAR keeps its members informed by offering a wide variety of educational programs; it also requires that they adhere to a strict code of ethics.

Although many people associate the word *REALTOR®* with all real estate agents, the term can only be used by brokers and agents who hold active membership in the association.

Approximately 30 percent of all real estate licensees in this country are REALTORS®.

Finding an Agent

To start your search for the right real estate agent, ask for referrals from friends, relatives, or coworkers who have had successful selling experiences. Then interview each potential agent.

If you can't get a referral, simply walk into any real estate office in your area and ask for an agent. Or drop in on some nearby open houses and talk to the agents there. Agents find that the open house is an effective way to publicize both homes for sale and themselves. When you walk into an open house, the agent on duty will likely try to solicit you as a client. The agent's expertise often shows during an open house, giving you some insight into his or her qualifications.

You can also get the names of brokers and agents from For Sale signs in your area. Pay particular attention to Sold signs. They can tell you something about an agency's track record. Finally, brokers and agents often are listed in the yellow pages and in advertisements in newspapers. In short, you won't have to worry too much about finding an agent—you will need to worry about finding a good one.

Once you've decided to put your house on the market, interview at least three local agents. Ask each of them to give you the names and telephone numbers of their three most recent sellers. Then phone these former clients and ask, "Were you in any way unhappy with the agent and would you work with him or her again?" You will soon know which agent should get your listing.

☞ **Money-$aving Tip #9** *Real estate brokers have a network of prospective buyers that will increase your chances for a faster sale and usually for a better price.*

The Interview

Once you have a few agents in mind, you can use the following questions as a way to sort through your choices:

- What is your educational background?
- How many years have you been active in the real estate business?
- Do you work as an agent full-time?
- Are you a member of the National Association of REALTORS®?
- Do you sell homes on a regular basis?
- Are you active in my neighborhood?
- Do you have recent references, people I can contact directly?
- Can I attend one of your open houses?
- Do you have access to the local MLS?
- What kind of marketing plan do you have?

After interviewing several agents, ask yourself this question: "Which one seems to be the type of person I want to represent me and my property?"

☞ **Money-$aving Tip #10** *Be sure the agent you select works full-time in the business. You want someone to be available whenever you or prospective buyers have any questions. And, it just seems logical that agents who do nothing but work in real estate will produce more than those who earn some of their income in other fields.*

☞ **Money-$aving Tip #11** *Your agent may give you a break on the commission if you use him or her to both list your home and find your next home.*

Remember: Before you list with an agent, be sure you get everything he or she will do for you down in writing.

How *Your Agent Can Help*

When you're ready to sell your home, you want the guidance and assistance of someone you can trust, who understands the complex elements of marketing and who is in touch with today's real estate market.

In short, you want to place your confidence in a qualified real estate professional who possesses the training, diligence and resources necessary to guide you through those important decisions you'll soon be making—but who also understands what your home really means to you.

When you list your home, a good agent will do the following:

- Provide the information you need to set the highest *realistic* price for your home.
- Prepare a detailed fact sheet highlighting the features and benefits of your home.
- Coordinate the efforts of other agents trying to sell your home.
- Generate prospective buyers with signs, ads, open houses and other proven sales techniques.
- Do his or her best to ensure that the prospective buyer for your home is qualified.
- Keep you informed of the number of showings to prospective buyers and their reactions to the house.
- Sign a guarantee of action; that is, that he or she will perform as promised.

The key to a successful sale is selecting the best real estate agent to market your home. A good real estate agent has the knowledge and skills to sell your home reasonably quickly and at the right price.

☞ **Money-$aving Tip #12** *The agent you choose could mean the difference between selling your house quickly for almost the full asking price, or selling the house a year from now at a reduced price.*

Commonly Asked Questions

Q. *Who does the real estate agent work for—the seller or the buyer?*

A. Real estate agents must disclose which party they represent. Traditionally they represent the seller, but buyer representation is a growing trend. An agent can represent both the seller and the buyer in dual representation (where legally allowed—check with your agent), but must have consent from both parties.

Q. *Who actually sells my house—the broker or the agent?*

A. Both. Legally, a real estate agent is a person trained and licensed to act for people who want to buy or sell a piece of property. While that definition applies to both broker and sales agent, only the broker is authorized to charge a fee or a commission, or both, for such services. The sales agent—who provides the legwork on a transaction—works on behalf of, and is compensated by, the broker. The broker furnishes supervision, backup resources and office expenses. Fees are shared between the broker and the sales agent according to a prearranged schedule; a 50/50 split is common.

Q. *Are real estate commissions negotiable?*

A. Yes. Commissions cannot be set by the real estate industry. The amount of a broker's commission is negotiable in every case. A broker can, however, set the minimum rate that is acceptable for that broker's firm.

Q. How many agents should I interview before I select one?

A. It is prudent to talk with at least three—even if you are pleased with the first one you meet. Allow each agent you interview to inspect your home and make his or her listing presentation.

CHAPTER 4

The Listing Process

Once you decide which broker to use, you will be asked to sign a contract giving the broker the right to list your home. By signing this contract, you agree to pay the broker a commission if your house is sold.

Types of Listings

A listing agreement is basically an employment contract. In most states, the listing must be in writing to be enforceable. However, oral listings are permitted in some jurisdictions.

There are several different types of listing agreements. Following are the most common ones:

Exclusive right to sell. In this type of agreement, the seller owes a commission even if he or she finds the buyer.

25

Brokers obviously favor this type of listing agreement because it gives them the protection they need to know that their time and effort will not go unrewarded.

Exclusive agency. You can sell the house on your own without paying a commission.

Multiple listing. A *multiple-listing* clause may be included in an exclusive listing. It gives the broker the authority and obligation to distribute the listing to other members of the broker's multiple-listing organization, thus exposing your house to a larger market. When the property is sold, the commission is divided between the listing broker and the selling broker.

Open. You can list with any number of brokers and pay commission only to the one who sells your home. You can also sell the house on your own without paying a commission.

Net. You pay the broker a commission equal to the difference between a specified sales price and the amount the broker can get for the home. Because net listings can create a conflict of interest between the broker's responsibility to the seller and the broker's profit motive, they are illegal in many states and are discouraged by real estate licensing authorities in most others.

☞ **Money-$aving Tip #13** *Make sure your broker agrees to list your house with the Multiple Listing Service in your area. Putting your home in the MLS will ensure that the property gets maximum exposure, which, in turn, will improve the chances that it will bring top dollar.*

Is the Commission Rate Carved in Stone?

Real estate commissions are entirely negotiable. Rates vary by region and usually range from 5 percent to 7 percent; the real estate industry cannot set the fee. How high a commission should you pay a broker? It depends on the services the broker offers. Some brokers put together a powerful promotional package and deserve a commission rate as high as 7 percent. Other brokers may offer to sell your house for a smaller percentage than the going rate, offering fewer services. Still others, called *discount brokers,* offer a limited number of real estate services—for a flat fee or a reduced commission—to those sellers who feel they can handle some of the work load themselves.

So how do you sort it all out? Be a comparison shopper. Compare the full-commission broker with the reduced-commission broker and make a decision based on services rendered rather than on the fee charged.

☞ **Money-$aving Tip #14** *Make a list of the names and addresses of any potential prospects with whom you've come in contact before deciding to use a broker. Then get your broker to agree to a reduced commission if someone on this list buys your house within the first month of its listing.*

How Long Should the Listing Agreement Run?

One of the most important things you will need to negotiate at the time of listing your house with a broker is the length of the listing agreement. Terms vary, but listing contracts are rarely written for less than three months or for more than one year.

It's a tough decision to make. You want to give the broker a long enough period as an incentive to spend the time, money and effort needed to sell your home. On the other hand, if you don't really know the broker, you want a relatively short agreement period in case things don't work out and you want to switch to someone else. Many experts agree that a listing of three months is enough time to satisfy both objectives. Then if the house doesn't sell within the period of the agreement, but you feel the broker has done a reasonably good job, you can always renew the listing. Additionally, you can request that a provision be added to the listing agreement whereby you can cancel the listing at any time if you are unhappy with the relationship. Keep in mind that the time of year can also be a factor. In markets with substantial seasonality, longer listing periods may be necessary if your house is being sold during the "off" season.

Caution: Be sure the listing agreement does not contain an automatic renewal clause. If you're not satisfied with your agent's performance, you will want to have the option of choosing someone else.

☞ **Money-Saving Tip #15** *When deciding on the length of the listing agreement, remember that, in general, homes that are competitively priced should sell within three months.*

Listing Agreement Form

A wide variety of listing contract forms are available today. Some brokers draft their own contracts, some use forms prepared by their Multiple Listing Service and some use forms produced by their state real estate licensing authority. But they all contain essentially the same information. An example of an *exclusive-right-to-sell* listing contract is shown in Figure 4.1.

A typical listing contract is a preprinted form that includes at least the following information:

Type of listing agreement. Is the contract an exclusive-right-to-sell listing, an exclusive-agency listing or an open listing? Is a multiple-listing clause included?

Names of all parties to the agreement. Anyone having an interest in the property must be identified and must sign the listing agreement for it to be valid.

Brokerage firm. The names of the brokerage company and of the agent taking the listing must be identified.

Length of agreement. Contract terms usually range from 90 to 180 days.

List price. The agreement should include the price you are asking for the house and the terms under which you will sell.

Your agent has several professional tools to provide information about your house's value and the selection of a realistic asking price, which will be covered in a later chapter.

Personal property. The contract should specify the personal property that will be included in the sale—appliances, fireplace accessories, drapes and so on.

Commission rate. The commission is based on the sales price of the home. The commission rate is negotiable.

Permissions. The contract should specify whether the broker can do such things as place a sign in the yard, use a lockbox, hold open houses and so on.

Broker protection clause. A protection clause states that the broker is entitled to a commission if a person to whom the broker has shown your house decides to buy after the listing has expired. This prevents the seller from waiting

FIGURE 4.1 Sample Listing Agreement

EXCLUSIVE RIGHT TO SELL LISTING AGREEMENT

TO: _____ (hereinafter "Agency") DATE: _____ , 19_____ .

In consideration of Agency's agreement to list and promote the sale of Seller's property located at _____

_____

recorded in the _____ County Registry of Deeds in Book _____ , Page _____ , the undersigned as Seller, hereby gives the Agency the exclusive right to sell or exchange said property at a price of $_____ , and on the terms herein stated, or at any other price or terms to which Seller may authorize or consent. If, during the term of this agreement, a Buyer is produced who is ready, willing and able to purchase at said price, or at any other price or terms to which the Seller may agree, or if the property is sold or exchanged by anyone, including the Seller, then Seller agrees to pay Agency a commission of _____% of contract price. This agreement shall be in effect for _____ months, from _____ , 19_____ to _____ , 19_____ .

The commission as provided above shall be due if the property is sold, conveyed, exchanged or otherwise transferred within _____ months (max. 6 months) after the expiration of this agreement to anyone with whom Agency has negotiated unless listed with another Agency on an Exclusive Right to Sell Listing Agreement. Negotiation shall include providing information about the property, showing the property, or presenting offers on the property. All rights under this paragraph shall terminate on _____ , 19_____ .

SUBAGENCY
☐ Yes   ☐ No   This Agency's policy is to cooperate with other agencies acting as subagents of you the Seller.
☐ Yes   ☐ No   This Agency's policy is to share compensation with subagents.

BUYER'S AGENCY
☐ Yes   ☐ No   This Agency's policy is to cooperate with other agencies acting as Buyer's agents.
☐ Yes   ☐ No   This Agency's policy is to share compensation with Buyer's agents.

Agency has disclosed its policies regarding cooperation and compensation so as to inform Seller of any policy that would limit the participation of any other Agency.

Agency and Seller each agree that this property is to be offered without regard to race, color, religion, sex, handicap/ disability, familial status (families with children), or national origin.

Seller acknowledges and/or agrees:
- A continuing duty between the signing of this listing agreement and the final closing to disclose to Agency all information about the property, adverse or otherwise, and understands that all such information shall be disclosed by Agency to Buyer.
- Seller holds Agency harmless for any claim which may result from the Seller's failure to disclose information about the property.
- To convey property by _____ deed.
- To authorize a "For Sale" sign on property.   ☐ Yes   ☐ No
- To authorize the advertising of property.   ☐ Yes   ☐ No
- To authorize publication of property in the MLS and use of information for marketing and statistical purposes.   ☐ Yes   ☐ No
- That State of Maine law requires Buyers of property owned by non-resident Sellers to withhold a prepayment of capital gains tax unless a waiver has been obtained by Seller from the State of Maine Bureau of Taxation.
- To seek legal, tax, and other professional advice as necessary in connection with sale of property.
- Receipt of a copy of this agreement.

Other Conditions: _____

_____

_____

SELLER(S) _____   _____
                                                                                        SS # OR TAXPAYER ID #

_____   _____
                                                                                        SS # OR TAXPAYER ID #

Accepted by _____   on behalf of _____
                              (Agent)   (Agency)

R REALTOR®   **Maine Association of REALTORS® /1994**
                              All Rights Reserved

out the listing and then making a deal with one of the broker's customers to cut the broker out of a commission. The contract should specify the length of time such a clause will remain in effect. Usually, the broker is protected for 90 days.

Marketing plan. The contract should spell out how the broker plans to market the house—through ads, fliers, open houses, MLS listing, TV, direct mail, the Internet and so on.

Multiple Listing Service. If your house is going to be listed through an MLS, this should be stated in the contract.

Homeowner warranty program. Is a home warranty plan available? What items does the warranty cover? Are you willing to pay for it? If not, will the plan be available to the buyer at the buyer's expense?

Equal opportunity clause. This clause states that the property must be shown and offered to all interested parties regardless of their race, color, creed or religion, national origin, sex, sexual orientation, age, handicap or source of income of the prospective buyer.

Description of the property. In addition to the street address, the property's legal description, lot size and tax parcel number are often listed for future insertion into a purchase offer.

Information about the property. Detailed information about the property, such as the number and sizes of the rooms and the size of the lot, may be included in the listing contract or on a separate property fact sheet, such as the one shown in Figure 4.2.

Because other people will be making important financial decisions based on the information contained in your listing or on your fact sheet, it is crucial that the details are accurate.

The closing. Who will handle the closing—a closing attorney, title company or escrow company?

Signatures of the parties. All parties identified in the contract must sign it.

☞ **Money-$aving Tip #16** *In most states, agreements with brokers must be in writing to be enforceable. So thank the broker for all the great things he or she is going to do for you—but then get them* in writing.

Fact Sheets

A fact sheet (see Figure 4.2) can be an effective marketing tool for your home. Because potential buyers typically look at 25 to 30 houses before they make a decision on which one to buy, a fact sheet is a way for them to jog their memories about your house's appearance and special features. Information on a fact sheet generally includes the following:

- A photograph of the house and lot
- The name of the owner(s)
- The street address of the property
- The broker or agent's name, address and telephone number
- The MLS number if the property has been entered into an MLS
- The dimensions of the lot
- The total square feet of living area
- The number and sizes of rooms
- The age of the house and type of construction
- Existing loans

FIGURE 4.2 Sample Fact Sheet

```
┌─────────────────────────────────────────────────────┐
│                              ┌──────────────────┐     │
│                              │                  │     │
│                              │  (Photo of home) │     │
│                              │                  │     │
│                              └──────────────────┘     │
│                                                       │
│  Address: _____  Price: _____       │
│  Style: _____  Taxes: _____       │
│  Entry: _____  Lot Size: _____       │
│  Living Room: _____   │
│  _____     │
│  Dining Room: _____   │
│  _____     │
│  Kitchen: _____   │
│  _____     │
│  Family Room/Den: _____   │
│  _____     │
│  Bedrooms: _____   │
│  _____     │
│  Bath: _____   │
│  _____     │
│  Basement: _____   │
│  Garage: _____   │
│  Special Features: _____   │
│  _____     │
│  Schools: _____   │
│  _____     │
│  Financing: _____   │
│  _____     │
│  Offered by: _____  Phone: _____      │
│  This information is believed to be accurate, but is   │
│  subject to errors, omissions, prior sale or          │
│  withdrawal.                                          │
└─────────────────────────────────────────────────────┘
```

- The possibility of seller financing
- The zoning classification of the property
- The current (or most recent year's) property taxes
- The neighborhood (schools, shopping, churches, public transportation, parks and recreation areas, etc.)
- Energy efficient items (fans, fireplace inserts, high-efficiency furnaces and water heaters, etc.)
- Any special features that make the property more appealing and marketable

☞ **Money-$aving Tip #17** *Time means money. To help sell your home faster, your agent should prepare a* fact sheet *about your house and neighborhood and distribute it to as many people as possible.*

Do You Need a Lawyer?

You are not required to have legal representation to sell a house; however, if you are going to hire a lawyer, you should do it early on—before you sign a listing agreement with a real estate broker. While a broker can handle most real estate transactions, he or she is not trained or licensed to give legal advice if something goes wrong.

If you prefer to work with an attorney, look for one who has extensive real estate experience. And don't hesitate to ask what the service will cost. An attorney will review contracts, point out potential problems and handle the closing for you.

If you don't know a real estate attorney, ask your agent for help. He or she can provide you with the names of competent attorneys in your area.

How *Your Agent Can Help*

Before you sign a listing agreement, a good agent will complete a written listing presentation. The presentation should include the following:

- Information about the agent and his or her firm
- Information about the housing market in your area—including the number of homes currently for sale and how many have recently sold
- A complete description of the features of your home
- Suggestions on what repairs to make and ways to improve curb appeal
- The agent's marketing plan
- A competitive pricing report on comparable homes to help you set a realistic asking price

Commonly Asked Questions

Q. Who determines the list price for my house?

A. Real estate agents suggest asking prices based on their knowledge, information and expertise. But it is ultimately you, the seller, who must determine the list price for your home.

Q. How long should it take to sell my house?

A. The length of time it takes to sell will vary, depending on market conditions, the price of the house, its location, terms and condition. But to get the best return from their marketing efforts, most real estate agents will tell you to allow a minimum of three months—six months when possible—before you expect to move.

Q. *What obligation am I under if I invite listing agents to my house?*

A. None. You are not obligated until you sign a listing contract.

Q. *Do I have to pay a commission if I find the buyer?*

A. It depends on the type of listing contract you sign. If you sign an exclusive-agency contract, you can sell the house on your own without paying a commission. But in an exclusive-right-to-sell listing, you owe a commission even if you find the buyer.

Q. *What is the advantage of an exclusive-right-to-sell listing?*

A. It protects the agent and gives him or her the incentive to work harder to sell the house quickly and at the right price.

CHAPTER 5

Having Your Home Professionally Inspected

A professional home inspection can alert you to problems that could complicate a potential sale. Correcting these problems early not only makes your property more desirable, but it also simplifies the negotiation process when the time comes for the buyer's prepurchase home inspection.

A buyer basically wants assurance that the house is structurally sound and its electrical and mechanical systems are in good condition. The American Society of Home Inspectors estimates that about half of all homes on the resale market have at least one significant defect, and nearly all homes need some maintenance and repair work.

Seller Disclosure

Homesellers who hide defects from buyers are asking for trouble. The principle of *caveat emptor*—let the buyer beware—doesn't apply anymore. As a result of recent court cases and new state laws, sellers are increasingly being asked to disclose known defects from the start. Sellers have long been liable for misrepresentations about major defects, including the withholding of information about hidden problems. And most states hold sellers responsible for any major defect they knew about or could reasonably have known about.

Under most state laws, sellers must tell buyers about any defect that may affect the value of the property; for example, a bad septic system, a leaky basement or a cracked foundation.

Adding to the burden on sellers are concerns over radon, lead, asbestos and other health threats. While no state requires sellers to test for such substances, the new laws generally require them to spell out what they know or don't know.

Appendix A shows a typical *disclosure statement* that many states now require a seller to complete. Disclosures have to be made at or prior to signing the sales contract. Two-thirds of all lawsuits against real estate brokers, agents or sellers in the United States allege misrepresentation or failure to disclose property defects. So to protect all parties involved in the sale of a house, including themselves, most brokers won't accept a listing without the seller first filling out a disclosure statement. By disclosing all of the property's defects, the seller is laying it all out on the table and the buyer has no reason to come back later and complain.

☞ **Money-$aving Tip #18** *To prevent the possibility of a lawsuit after the sale, get the buyer's written acknowledgment of any major problems before you accept an offer.*

The Professional Home Inspector

To help them provide full disclosure, some sellers are now paying for a professional home inspection at the time of listing. A typical inspection report is shown in Appendix B. This report can be shown to prospective buyers to assure them that all known defects are being disclosed. The last thing a seller wants is for a buyer to come back after a sale and claim there is a defect in the property that the seller didn't reveal.

A home inspection should cover foundations and basement slabs, roofing, walls, ceilings, floors, windows and doors. An inspector will determine whether main structural components are sound, free from rot or insect damage, and strong enough to support the weight of the house.

The inspector will check out all exposed water and waste pipes, faucets, drainage, water heaters and connections to appliances. The inspector will also evaluate the overall condition of the electrical system to see that it's adequate for current and future needs.

Grounding connections and exposed wiring will be tested for overload protection, and heating and cooling systems will be tested for efficiency.

Home inspectors look for termite damage, but some are not licensed to evaluate whether termites are present. A termite report, sometimes required by a financial institution before it will issue a mortgage, should come from a licensed pest-control company.

A typical home inspection generally does not include looking for environmental hazards—the presence of contaminants in water, radon gas, leaking underground storage tanks, asbestos, lead paint or urea foam insulation, to name a few. An environmental assessment of the property must be made by someone trained to identify and test for potential environmental hazards.

A home inspection typically costs between $200 and $400 for an evaluation of the mechanical and structural components of a home and, if needed, another $200 to $300 for a formal environmental assessment.

☞ **Money-$aving Tip #19** *In today's market, little things can mean a lot. Having written evidence that a house is in good shape could tip a buyer in your direction—resulting in a quicker sale at the right price.*

Take a Tour with the Inspector

Try to accompany the inspector during the examination. You may learn some things about the house that won't make it to the written report. Although you should maintain a low profile during the inspection, don't be afraid to ask questions. And, above all, don't push the panic button if the inspector finds some problems. Remember, no house is perfect. If you know early on about defects that could possibly cloud a sale, you'll have time to deal with them before an interested buyer comes along.

☞ **Money-$aving Tip #20** *It can pay to have your house inspected before listing—particularly if you know it needs some work. That way, if there are any serious problems, you can have them corrected at your convenience. And, you have time to shop around for the best possible price.*

How Do You Find a Good Home Inspector?

A home inspector can be an engineer, an architect, a builder or someone else with solid experience. In selecting a competent home inspector, look for one who belongs to a professional home inspection organization, such as the American Society of Home Inspectors, which requires its members to meet certain standards of education and experience. Real estate agents can help also by referring you to qualified inspectors in the area.

Here are some questions to ask the inspectors you contact:

- How long have you been in the business?
- What is your training and background?
- What certification(s) do you have?
- Are you specifically experienced in residential construction?
- Is your company free of any repair or real estate connections that might cause a conflict of interest?
- What will the inspection include and how long will it take?
- How much will the inspection cost?

☞ **Money-$aving Tip #21** *Avoid home inspectors who also do repair work or recommend contractors. You want someone who has nothing to gain by finding defects in the house.*

☞ **Money-$aving Tip #22** *If an inspection reveals major, costly problems, you can offer to reduce your price to compensate for them rather than take on the expense before selling.*

How *Your Agent Can Help*

Having your property professionally inspected before you list it can pay off. Buyers like the idea, and it gives you time to decide what to do about a problem before the buyer finds it. Your agent should be able to give you the names of qualified home inspectors in your area. Some real estate firms can also arrange for deferred-payment inspections.

Anyone selling a house has the duty to disclose defects. Your agent can help you fill out the seller disclosure statement—if one is required in the state in which your property is located.

Commonly Asked Questions

Q. Is it the job of the professional home inspector to tell the seller whether he or she thinks the house is worth its asking price?

A. No. The inspector's job is to describe the condition of the house and make the seller aware of repairs and replacements that are recommended or necessary—not how much the house is worth.

Q. What's an inspection clause?

A. A stipulation in a sales contract that makes the agreement contingent on the findings of a professional home inspector.

Q. What is a homeowner's responsibility concerning disclosures?

A. Homeowners must be honest about any defects they know of that their property has. These problems most likely will be discovered during the buyer's inspection anyway. And the courts have held that sellers must disclose known facts that may affect the value of the property.

Q. What happens if the seller is aware of problems, but chooses not to disclose them?

A. The seller could be exposed to a lawsuit arising from fraudulent misrepresentations.

Q. What is the best way for a seller and real estate agent to protect themselves from future liability to a buyer?

A. You need to fully disclose in writing all known defects in the home and then sell the property "as is."

Q. Why do I need a home inspection?

A. Basically for your own protection, and to make your home more salable. Real estate agents, knowing that nondisclosure of defects can lead to costly lawsuits, have come to view home inspections as an important part of buying and selling a home.

CHAPTER 6

Preparing Your Home for Sale

Once you put your house on the market, you have to get it ready to be presented to potential buyers. Preparing your home for sale doesn't have to mean making costly additions or remodeling. Most buyers looking for a home will want to plan their own major changes. All that's necessary may be cleaning, painting, landscape maintenance and minor repairs.

The closer to impeccable your home is, the easier it will be to show and to sell. While major remodeling projects, with some exceptions, usually don't pay, minor repairs and cosmetic touches generally do. Overall, your goal should be to make it as easy as possible for buyers to imagine themselves living in the home. If the interior of your house includes a lot of personal decorating touches, change them for more conservative themes and colors.

☞ **Money-$aving Tip #23** *Making simple repairs and carrying out thorough cleaning and maintenance chores— none of which calls for significant spending—can add value to a home and make the difference between a quick sale at the desired asking price and a lengthy one at a lowered price.*

Curb Appeal

First impressions are critical when it comes to swaying buyers and getting them excited about purchasing your home. Real estate agents recognize the importance of the first impression and refer to it as *curb appeal.* Put another way, curb appeal is the term for everything prospective buyers can see from the street that might make them want to turn in and take a closer look at a house for sale.

Imagine yourself as the buyer and view your lot from across the street to get an overall impression of the landscaping, driveway, walks, patios, decks, fences and any other structures on the property. All of these things contribute to the overall appearance of the house and, depending on their condition, can play a big part in how quickly and at what price your house sells.

Landscaping

Landscaping has a lot to do with curb appeal. A poorly maintained landscape will turn buyers off even before they enter the house. So keep the grass cut, edge the driveway and front walk, weed the flower beds, trim the hedges and rake up the leaves to improve curb appeal and generate more buyer traffic.

☞ **Money-$aving Tip #24** *Simple, but neat, landscaping can help the marketability of your house.*

How Does the House Look on the Outside?

What is the first impression of the house? Does the outside need painting? Does the entranceway make an appealing impression? An attractive entranceway makes a positive statement each time your house is shown; it's one of the first things potential buyers notice.

How does the roof look? Are there any missing shingles? Are the gutters and downspouts in place? Is the siding in good condition? If a house looks rundown on the outside, home shoppers will just assume it's rundown on the inside. Remember, even a broken mailbox can give your home a neglected look. But if the home is neat and clean on the outside, potential buyers will see a well-cared-for home that looks easy to maintain. Your home on the outside should look as if you've maintained it well over the years.

Even the finest interior design can be wasted if attention is not paid to the exterior of your house. Nothing compares to curb appeal. Figure 6.1 features a list of things to do to help you keep the outside of your property at peak value.

☞ **Money-$aving Tip #25** *The wise homeowner will improve the lot and outside appearance of the house before it is put up for sale. It makes dollars and it makes sense.*

What to Do on the Inside of the House

Inside the home, neatness and an impression of spaciousness and light are crucial. A house that doesn't show well has little chance of selling quickly and for a good price. Figure 6.2 is a list of things for you to do to make the inside of your home more presentable for sale.

Pay particular attention to the last item in Figure 6.2—when the agent is showing your home, make yourself scarce. Prospective buyers have an easier time of it when

FIGURE 6.1 Outside Checklist

❏ Keep the lawn mowed and edged, hedges trimmed and the yard uncluttered.

❏ Keep driveway, walks and steps free of ice, snow, leaves and debris.

❏ Repair the roof if needed—fix leaks and replace any loose or missing shingles.

❏ Repair or replace leaky gutters and downspouts.

❏ Paint and repair roof overhangs if needed.

❏ Paint and repair siding if needed.

❏ Repair potholes in blacktop and large cracks in concrete.

❏ Fix and paint fence if needed.

❏ Fix and paint wood deck if needed.

❏ Place special emphasis on the front entry. Paint the front door; lubricate the hinges and handle; polish metal items such as brass knobs or address numbers; repair and paint any porch railings; make sure the doorbell and outdoor lighting fixtures work; and buy a new, unobtrusive welcome mat.

the owner's not around. It's hard for buyers to imagine that this could be their house when you, the owner, are watching every move they make. If you do stick around to answer questions, stay uninvolved—and let the agent do the selling.

☞ **Money-$aving Tip #26** *When your house is scheduled to be shown, put your valuables in a safe place. Even though an agent should escort any prospective buyer through your home, don't leave money, jewelry or other valuables out in the open.*

FIGURE 6.2 Inside Checklist

Before Showing the House

❏ Paint walls and ceilings if needed. Neutral colors appeal to most potential buyers.

❏ Shampoo carpeting.

❏ Clean and wax bare floors.

❏ Replace stained or torn wallpaper.

❏ Remove stains from bathroom and kitchen counters, fixtures and so on.

❏ Make the kitchen appear bright and attractive. The kitchen is the most important room in the house. If cabinets are dull, consider painting them. Put up perky new curtains. Also consider increasing brightness by using bulbs of higher wattage.

❏ Fix sticky windows and drawers.

❏ Repair broken windows.

❏ Oil creaky door hinges.

❏ Fix or replace any doors that do not open or close easily.

❏ Repair leaky faucets and clogged drains.

❏ Repair leaks underneath sinks and repair damage from previous leaks.

❏ Replace broken or missing hardware on doors, windows and cabinets.

❏ Make sure all mechanical systems and appliances are in good working condition. Make repairs where needed.

❏ Clean out the attic and garage.

❏ Remove oil stains from garage floor.

❏ Avoid clutter. Neatness makes a room look bigger.

FIGURE 6.2 Inside Checklist (Continued)

When the House Is Scheduled to Be Shown

❑ Keep the temperature at a comfortable level.

❑ Keep window draperies and shades open to let in light, to show a pleasant view, if any, and to make rooms appear larger.

❑ Dust thoroughly.

❑ Keep the house well ventilated and fresh smelling.

❑ Eliminate any pet odors.

❑ Place flowers and touches of greenery throughout the house.

❑ Have a crackling fire on a cold winter day.

❑ Keep kitchen spotless.

❑ Keep bathrooms clean and neat. And put fresh towels on the towel rods.

❑ Keep closets and storage spaces clean and uncluttered.

❑ Keep windows and mirrors clean.

❑ Keep floors scrubbed and vacuumed.

❑ Keep on soft music and freshly bake cookies or bread to make the house seem more inviting.

❑ Let the real estate agent show your house and don't tag along.

Should You Make Any Major Home Improvements?

Certain home improvements that are useful to most people have been proven to add value and, in some cases, even speed the sale of houses (see Appendix B). These include building a deck or patio, finishing a basement, cosmetic or minor kitchen remodeling (refinishing cabinets and countertops, new oven and cooktop, etc.), changing floor and wall coverings, especially in bathrooms, and, in warmer climates, adding central air-conditioning.

Improvements that return far less than what they cost are usually things that appeal to personal tastes, such as adding skylights, swimming pools and wet bars, or converting the attic into an extra room.

☞ **Money-$aving Tip #27** *The most cost-effective improvements are to the kitchen or bathroom.*

The difficulty that comes with any home improvement designed to help sell your house is determining whether you can recoup your investment. There's always the risk of over-improving your house—that is, putting more money into it than neighborhood prices will support.

So how much is too much? Real estate professionals suggest that you keep the value of your property within 15 to 20 percent of others in your neighborhood. If you live in a neighborhood of $100,000 homes, buyers shopping your area probably want a home close to that price. Buyers who can afford pricier homes will shop in more expensive areas.

If you live in an area where real estate prices are low and unchanging, be especially cautious about overimprovement. Without the prospect of rising prices ahead, buyers may be reluctant to exceed neighborhood norms. In low-price markets, even a modest remodeling may overimprove your home from a resale standpoint. That's why you might want to ask your agent's opinion about the viability of recovering the cost on any major remodeling project you have in mind before you start the work.

To improve your chances of a good return, style your remodeling for mass appeal. Buyers prefer neutral, mainstream design, so play it safe with colors and materials. And keep your remodeling compatible with the existing house. Choose materials and design elements that match—or at least blend—with what's already there.

☞ **Money-Saving Tip #28** *Improvements that bring a home up to par with a neighborhood earn a better return than those that put it above the rest.*

How Your Agent Can Help

First impressions are often lasting impressions. So, your home should be in top condition before it is placed on the market. A good real estate agent will view your house with an impartial eye and offer valuable suggestions for showing your home at its best. A neat, well-maintained house and simple, inexpensive improvements can add thousands of dollars to a home's value and increase the chances of a quick, profitable sale.

Commonly Asked Questions

Q. How much should I spend getting my house ready for sale?

A. Spend as little as possible. First, give your house a good scrubbing and get rid of all the clutter. Then correct any cosmetic flaws you've noticed to improve visual appeal. Finally, make sure that everything is in working order, inside and outside.

Q. Should I make any major home improvements?

A. Don't spend serious money on an improvement unless you can recoup your investment; or if the improvement will take care of a significant deficiency—an outdated kitchen, for example. Ask your agent for advice on the kinds of improvements that will improve the salability of your home.

Q. Should I be around when an agent brings a prospective buyer to see the house?

A. Probably not. Buyers often feel uncomfortable speaking candidly and asking questions in front of the homeowner.

Q. Can I expect a report from my agent about the showing?

A. A good agent should always give the seller a frank report on a prospective buyer's reaction to the house. Buyer comments can help you make the kinds of changes that will improve your chances of selling the home within a reasonable timeframe. In addition, your agent should follow up with other agents who have shown the home and give you any feedback on the comments and reactions of their prospective buyers as well.

CHAPTER 7

How Much
Is It Worth?

While emotional attachment can make a house a home, the actual value of a house depends on many factors. These include the neighborhood in which the house is located, the condition of the house, current market conditions, interest rates and the length of time the house has been for sale.

Who is valuing it and why also affect the worth of a home. Homebuyers, homesellers, mortgage lenders, insurance companies and tax authorities all have different points of view about the value of a home.

How can you determine the actual value of a home? First, your real estate agent can give you a good estimate of the home's value by doing a competitive market analysis (CMA). This means analyzing housing demands in the neighborhood, recent sales of similar properties and the availability of financing. Having an appraisal done by a professional appraiser is another way. This opinion or estimate of value is not a statement of fact. As a result, it might be subject to honest dispute. Nevertheless, an appraisal by an experienced professional comes as close to an objective evaluation as you can get. Also, financial institutions insist on an appraisal to determine the amount of money they will lend to a credit applicant.

What Is a Real Estate Appraisal?

In theory, at least, appraising is a simple concept to grasp. An appraisal is a supportable estimate of property value. It includes a description of the property under consideration and the appraiser's opinion of the property's condition, its utility for a given purpose and/or its probable monetary value on the open market. Because it is only an estimate, the worth of any appraisal depends on the skill, experience and good judgment of the person making the appraisal. With an objective, well-researched and carefully documented appraisal, all parties involved, whether in a sale, a proposed mortgage loan or other transaction, are assisted in the decision-making process.

To produce a reasonably accurate estimate of value, the appraiser must compile all relevant data, assemble it in an orderly manner, and use standard procedures and techniques developed through the experience of the appraisal profession. Thus, an appraisal is a combination of fact findings, sound judgment and past experience. An appraiser will thoroughly inspect your home's exterior and interior, paying close attention to the heating, air-conditioning, plumbing and electrical wiring systems. If any major flaws are found, the appraiser will often recommend that a specialist be brought in to inspect the defect.

In addition, the professional appraiser will consider the location of your property and its proximity to stores, schools and recreational areas. All environmental factors in the neighborhood are evaluated, as well as traffic, parking facilities, zoning laws, trends in property taxes and general market conditions. In the final value estimate, neighborhood analysis is as important as the special characteristics of the property itself.

The appraiser may spend only a few hours actually inspecting your property, but will spend considerable time researching data, collecting information from legal records, checking sales of comparable houses and accumulating other pertinent information necessary to estimate your home's value.

To find out what your property is worth, the appraiser acts as a disinterested third party; his or her compensation is not contingent on the amount of the value estimate. With no financial interest in the property and nothing to gain or lose from the outcome of the appraisal, the appraiser should be able to objectively evaluate the property's relative merits, appeal and value.

☞ **Money-$aving Tip #29** *An appraisal can be a valuable bargaining tool during contract negotiations because most buyers view it as an impartial, almost scientific proof of value.*

Sales Comparison Approach

The sales comparison approach is used for almost every appraisal situation, but is particularly reliable in valuing single-family residences. In the sales comparison approach, an estimate of value is obtained by comparing the property being appraised—the *subject property*—to recent sales of similar, nearby properties, called *comparables* or *comps* for short. The theory is that the value of the subject property is related directly to the sales prices of the comparable properties.

The objective of the sales comparison approach is to estimate the *market value* of the subject property. Market value is the most probable price a property should bring in a sale occurring under normal market conditions. The market value estimate is based on actual sales of comparable properties. The appraiser must collect, classify, analyze and interpret a body of market data.

The rationale of the sales comparison approach is that a knowledgeable buyer will not pay more for a property than the cost to acquire a comparable alternative property.

To implement the sales comparison approach, the appraiser finds three to five or more properties that have been sold recently and are similar to the subject property. The appraiser notes any dissimilar features and makes an adjustment for each by using the following formula:

Sales Price of ± Adjustments = Indicated Value of
Comparable   Subject Property
Property

Adjustments are made to the sales price of a comp by *adding* the value of features present in the subject property but not in the comp and *subtracting* the value of features present in the comp but not in the subject property.

The adjusted sales prices of the comps represent the probable value range of the subject property. From this range, a single market value estimate can be selected.

Major types of adjustments include those made for physical condition and features of the house and lot, locational differences, conditions of the sale (buyer-seller motivation and financing terms) and the time from the date of the sale.

Example

- House A, the subject property, has central air-conditioning and a garage.

- A comparable property, house B, sold for $100,000 one month before the time of the appraisal. House B has a garage but no central air-conditioning, which is valued at $3,000.
- House C is comparable to the subject property and sold recently for $95,000. House C has central air-conditioning but no garage, which is valued at $7,000.
- House D, also comparable to the subject property, sold recently for $114,000. It has both a garage and central air-conditioning. House D, however, is located in a better area of the neighborhood than the subject is. The location adjustment is valued at $10,000.

A summary of the adjustment information is as follows:

Comparable Sales Chart
Comparables

	B	C	D
Sales price	$100,000	$95,000	$114,000
Location			–10,000
Garage		+7,000	
Air-conditioning	+3,000		
Adjusted sales price	$103,000	$102,000	$104,000

The value of house A, the subject property, will fall within the price range of the adjusted comparable properties; that is, between $102,000 and $104,000.

The accuracy of an appraisal using the sales comparison approach depends on the appraiser's use of reliable adjustment values.

☞ **Money-$aving Tip #30** *To get a top valuation, make sure your home is in "show condition."*

How Does the CMA Work?

The *competitive market analysis* (CMA) is a variation of the sales comparison approach, but is not as comprehensive or technical.

Similar to the sales comparison approach, the real estate agent doing a CMA will compare the prices of recently sold properties that are similar in location, style and amenities to your property. Then, adjustments are made for any significant differences between your property and the comparable properties. Based on the results of the CMA, your agent will derive a market value range and ultimately a competitive list price for your house. Appendix C shows a typical competitive market analysis form.

Following are some of the factors your agent will consider when analyzing comparable properties to derive a list price for your property:

Type of market. Is it a buyer's or a seller's market? To what degree and for how long? Answers to these questions will tell the real estate agent how difficult it will be to sell the property.

Price movement. Are prices dropping, holding steady or moving up? This is an indicator of where to price the home in the range of values.

Demand for features. Are the major features of the house in high, medium or low demand? When you combine the ratings of all the major features, it will indicate the difficulty of selling the home and therefore how to rate it for pricing.

Supply of homes. How long will it take to sell the existing inventory of similar properties? This fact, combined with how long the seller has to sell, will indicate the property's appropriate price range; that is, high, medium or low.

Days on market. This tells the agent the average length of time it will take to sell the property. This, compared with the length of time the seller has to sell, is another indicator of price.

Interest rates. Will the change in interest rates increase buyers in the market, reduce them or keep them at current levels? Anticipating the future gives the agent another indicator of asking price.

Feature comparison of current competition. Feature for feature, how does your house stack up against what buyers will see when making comparisons? The list price will affect the buyer's justification for making an offer.

By analyzing and interpreting each of these factors, your agent can come up with a reasonable list price for your home; that is, whether the list price should be set at the high end, in the middle or at the low end of the value range.

Setting the List Price

Perhaps the most common mistake sellers make in today's market is clinging to yesterday's prices. What your neighbors paid for their home several years ago, or even last year, is not relevant to the sale of your home today. By asking too much initially, you may waste the critical first 30 to 45 days of the listing period. Your freshly spruced-up home will look its best in those early weeks and it will be shown more. If you lose those potential buyers, you will have to wait for a new crop of prospects to trickle in.

Your real estate agent is your best source of information on pricing your home. Ask him or her to prepare a competitive market analysis to help you position your home in the correct price range. This analysis will help you accurately compare your home against similar homes in your neighborhood. It's a valuable tool that will help you determine a realistic asking price for your property.

Generally speaking, the list price of a house when it goes on the market is set slightly higher than market value. Because most buyers expect to pay less than the asking price, you can assume that some negotiation will be necessary to reach an agreement. In most cases, the agent will go over the results of your CMA with you and help you establish a competitive pricing strategy.

A word of caution: Stay away from real estate agents who simply ask you what price you want for your home and agree to list it at that price. This practice can be in conflict with your best interests. By setting an unrealistically high list price, you could greatly extend the length of time it takes to sell your home. In fact, a house that is put on the market at too high a price often develops "market shyness," making it very difficult to sell; and you could end up getting even less than the fair market value of your home.

The basic point is that if, for example, several agents tell you the most your house will probably sell for is $90,000 and someone else tells you that he or she can get you $110,000, don't jump for joy that at last you have found the one agent who sees what the others have missed.

☞ **Money-$aving Tip #31** *When setting the price on your home, leave room for negotiation. Set the price slightly higher than fair market value. Most buyers expect to pay less than the asking price.*

Getting an Appraisal

In most cases, a CMA is all that's needed to determine a fair price for your home. You may also consider having an appraisal done as a double check—especially if you and your agent are not in agreement on what the house is worth. An appraised property is attractive to buyers, particularly those from out of the area, who aren't familiar with local prices and need reassurance that they are not overpaying. In fact, statistics show that appraised homes, in general, sell faster.

Why Pricing Is Important

Lending institutions base their loans on the appraised value of properties—not on the selling price. Assume this scenario: A buyer agrees to pay $100,000 for a house and is looking for a conventional 80 percent loan that requires a 20 percent down payment. Based on the $100,000 value, the mortgage loan would be $80,000 ($100,000 × .80) and the down payment would be $20,000 ($100,000 − $80,000). Now, suppose the lender's appraiser comes along and says the house is worth only $90,000. The seller and the buyer may have agreed that the house is worth $100,000. But if the lender's appraiser disagrees, the seller has a problem. The mortgage loan will be offered on the basis of the appraiser's estimate. The buyer would get a loan of $72,000 ($90,000 × .80) and would have to make a down payment of $28,000 ($100,000 − $72,000)—or $8,000 more. If the buyer isn't able (or willing) to put that much down, this can mark the death knell of the deal.

The caveat here is that a seller must be realistic about the value of his or her property and price it accordingly. Otherwise, a buyer may have a difficult time obtaining financing. The result is a lost sale and a lot of wasted time on both sides.

☞ **Money-$aving Tip #32** *Price it right if you want a quick sale. Be sure your asking price is competitive with those of similar properties in your neighborhood.*

☞ **Money-$aving Tip #33** *If your house has remained on the market for six months or more without selling, chances are you've overpriced it. Take it off the market for a few weeks. It's probably what real estate people call a "tired listing" anyhow. During that time, take a fresh look at your house and the competition and try to determine why it hasn't sold.*

How *Your Agent Can Help*

Real estate agents can find out what your home is worth in today's market, without obligation. They will analyze housing demands in your area, recent sales of similar properties, the availability of financing and more to determine the value of your home.

To serve as a further check on your home's market value, you can have it professionally appraised for a relatively inexpensive fee. Your agent can give you the names of reliable appraisers in your area.

Commonly Asked Questions

Q. *What is meant by* fair market value?

A. The most probable price an informed buyer will pay for real estate, assuming normal market conditions.

Q. What is meant by competitive market analysis?

A. A comparison of the prices of recently sold homes that are similar to a listing seller's home in terms of location, style and amenities.

Q. Do I need a professional appraisal?

A. An appraisal can be useful, especially if you and your agent disagree on the market value of the house; it can also be a helpful bargaining tool in contract negotiations, because most buyers accept an appraisal as an impartial proof of value.

Most sellers, however, rely on their agents' competitive market analyses to determine a market value range for the house.

Q. What should I do if I need to sell quickly?

A. Don't experiment with the price. You can increase your chances for a quick sale by listing the house below fair market value right from the start. How far below market value you set the asking price will depend on how urgent it is for you to sell quickly.

Q. What if the lender's appraiser doesn't find my house worth at least the amount of the sales price?

A. The lending institution will refuse to base its loan on that price. So, depending on the wording of the agreement, the buyer may have the right to back out of the deal. Or the contract can be renegotiated; often, a compromise can be worked out, with each side giving up something.

Q. What is at the top of the list of things that can kill a sale?

A. Most real estate agents will agree that overpricing is the single biggest factor in killing a sale. That's why they do a competitive market analysis on a home before working with the seller to set a competitive price.

Q. How important is my agent's list price recommendation?

A. Very important. Your agent has a variety of information at his or her disposal, including recent listing and selling prices of similar houses in your neighborhood, to help you estimate fair market value and set the highest realistic price for your home. But if you're not completely satisfied with your agent's suggestions, you may want to order a professional real estate appraisal.

CHAPTER 8

Marketing
Your Home

An effort to attract buyers to a house for sale should come after it has been put in top-notch condition and has been priced in line with the market. Remember that few things turn prospective buyers off as fast as a house that has cosmetic or maintenance deficiencies. And, don't challenge reality. A home is worth only so much. If you set the price too high, buyers will avoid your property. If you set the price too low, you'll get less than the value you deserve.

Getting the Attention of Buyers

In today's real estate marketplace, homes aren't sold, they're marketed. Your agent should provide you with a plan for marketing your house—that is, attracting buyers. No matter how fantastic your home is, it's not going to sell unless buyers know it is available. This chapter discusses some marketing strategies used by real estate brokers and agents.

For Sale Sign

One of the first steps your agent will take to market your home is to put up a sign. It tells people driving through the neighborhood that your house is for sale.

The For Sale sign should be professionally designed, attractive, neat and easily read. Many signs now include small boxes to hold fact sheets that describe the property.

Placing Ads

Advertising remains one of the most important components of the marketing process. So, without question, your real estate agent will want to advertise your home in the local newspaper as well as in other publications, such as real estate booklets of homes for sale that are available free of charge in grocery stores and other locations.

An effective ad triggers an emotional response from a prospective buyer that results in a phone call. This, in turn, gives the agent a chance to identify the prospect, determine his or her needs, and try to turn the prospect into a buyer.

You should always review ads and other marketing materials to be sure that information about your property is accurate. At the same time, you may want to make suggestions to the agent. After all, who knows your house and its best features better than you?

Here are some guidelines to help you evaluate newspaper ads:

- Does the ad attract and hold the reader's attention?
- Does the ad convey valuable and useful information without being overly cute or clever?
- Is the ad honest? One of the biggest complaints of prospective buyers is misrepresentation in some real

estate ads. An ad should not build up expectations in the mind of a prospect that cannot be fulfilled.

- Are the amenities and the positive aspects of a home undersold by placing too much emphasis on price?
- Is the ad written in such a way that the reader perceives your home satisfying his or her needs?
- Have abbreviations been overused, reducing the effectiveness of the ad? If abbreviations are used, make sure that they are well recognized by the potential readers of the ad.
- Does the ad overuse superlatives? Regardless of the quality of the home and the value being offered, it should not be so oversold in the ad that the prospective buyer will be disappointed when he or she sees it.
- Be sure the ad contains no reference to race, religion, creed, national origin, sexual preference, marital status or mental or physical disability.

Although brokers spend more money on advertising than on any other marketing tool, it accounts for no more than one-third of the sales. Most sales come from referrals or other contacts, signs in the yard and the broker's accumulation of potential buyers.

☞ **Money-$aving Tip #34** *If you are selling your home yourself, avoid using words such as* handyman special, price reduced *or* owner anxious *in your ads. They devalue your marketing position by suggesting to buyers that you need to sell quickly and that you'll accept just about any kind of offer. If you are using a real estate agent, be sure he or she solicits your input.*

The Open House

The open house is another critical part of the marketing process. Usually held on a Saturday or Sunday afternoon, it allows prospective buyers to view houses in a low-pressure, relaxed atmosphere. With that in mind, it isn't expected to generate a sale—at least not directly. What your agent looks for is traffic. Your agent will give you a full report on open house activity and offer an assessment of its results.

Real estate agents also hold an open house for other agents soon after a house is listed. The idea behind this is that the more agents who see your house, the more exposure it gets and the more prospective buyers you're likely to reach.

The agent's responsibility. Answering the phone, safeguarding property, controlling traffic flow through the house, answering appropriate questions and pointing out desirable features of the home all fall under the real estate agent's responsibilities during an open house. Locking up or removing valuables prior to the open house is the seller's job.

Homeowners should stage a walkthrough with an eye toward items that are obviously expensive and easily transportable. Anything that turns heads should be concealed.

☞ **Money-$aving Tip #35** *By holding too many open houses, you may overexpose your home and create the impression that it is difficult to sell.*

Word-of-Mouth Advertising

In a market like today's, you need to take advantage of every opportunity to sell your house. Get the word out. Even though your agent is responsible for getting your home sold, don't be shy about letting people know that your home is for sale. Some houses *do* get sold through word of mouth.

To sell property, you need to get the word out to as many people as possible—even people with no apparent interest in your home. Why? Because these people may have friends, relatives or coworkers who want a home just like yours. Spread the word to your neighbors, to all your friends and acquaintances, and to apartment renters and business people in the area. Almost anything you can do to boost the odds in your favor is worth the effort.

The Fact Sheet

Another useful aid in selling a house is the fact sheet. Your agent should prepare a fact sheet that describes your property, its special virtues and the price you want. Because buyers are shown so many houses these days, a fact sheet can function both as a memory aid and as a safety check to make sure they know who to contact for any additional information about the house. For a sample fact sheet, refer back to Figure 4.2.

Make sure the information on the fact sheet is absolutely accurate. An inaccurate fact sheet has the potential to cause trouble. It could be used as evidence that you or your agent misled the buyer.

A special kind of fact sheet is the MLS entry. Your agent will take down the key information about your home, including price, terms, location, size, special features and much more.

Sales Incentives

The real estate market varies substantially depending on your location. However, current interest rates are low, and there are steps you can take to add luster to a home for sale.

When the real estate market is slow, more creative marketing ideas are needed. The key to success is to start with inexpensive and risk-free enticements, then follow up as you need to with more complex strategies to custom-design an approach that will sell your house.

Work with your agent to design a marketing package that will increase the odds that buyers will want to look at your house rather than the competition's. For buyers strapped for cash, you might offer to help with closing costs; or you can offer to pay their principal and interest for several months. Buyers like the idea of living for free while you pick up the tab. You can treat it as a reduction in price for tax purposes.

To help a buyer qualify for a mortgage, you might consider a mortgage *buydown,* in which you offer to pay the lender a flat sum to lower the interest rate on the buyer's mortgage. Buydowns can be a powerful selling tool. They aren't complicated, and you avoid the risks of lending directly.

Buydowns can work better than cutting your asking price because buyers get a double benefit—a cheaper mortgage and the ability to qualify for a larger loan.

You can treat the cost of the buydown as a drop in the sales price. This will reduce the commission you pay to the real estate agent (your contract should specify a fee based on the net sales price) and the taxable gain on the house.

Buyers with plenty of cash from the sale of a previous home may be less impressed with financial incentives, but may be open to other enticements. Say, for example, a buyer comes along who loves your house but hates the carpet and can't stand the wallpaper. You might want to offer a decorating allowance—to be paid at closing—covering agreed-upon redecorating expenses.

A home warranty policy is worth investigating. This protects the major systems and appliances in the house for up to a year. The last thing a new homeowner wants to worry about is shelling out more cash for a costly home repair. A home warranty may make an older home more attractive to a buyer.

☞ **Money-$aving Tip #36** *If your house isn't selling as quickly as you'd like, ask your agent to quiz other agents about the objections their prospective buyers have mentioned, and then try to address the more relevant issues.*

Seller Financing

When your house won't sell, you may want to offer the buyer financing help. But be very cautious! Seller financing can be risky.

You may provide all of the financing or just part of the purchase price—which is the usual case. This can be inviting to a buyer with little cash for a down payment. While seller financing means attracting more potential buyers, the downside is that the bank holds the first mortgage and has a primary claim should the buyer default.

If you do decide to take on some of the financing

- get a credit report on the buyer;
- have your attorney draft an agreement;
- get at least the going rate of interest; and
- keep the term of the loan as short as possible.

Try an Auction

If you absolutely have to sell, and soon, consider putting your house up for auction. Traditionally reserved for foreclosures and tax sales, auctions can be just another way to market real estate, especially when things are slow.

There are two basic types of auctions: *absolute* and *reserve.* In an absolute auction, whoever has the highest bid wins—even if the highest bid is ridiculously low. A reserve auction gives the seller an out. Here the auctioneer and seller have set a minimum price and if the highest bid exceeds this price, the property is sold. If the highest bid is below the minimum or reserve value, then the seller has the right to reject the offer and take the property off the market.

Real estate auctioneers target buyers through carefully placed advertising that usually runs two weeks before the sale. They also put up large signs on the property itself or on major thoroughfares leading to the property. In addition, auctioneers use their extensive mailing lists to reach buyers who have expressed an interest in the type of property being offered.

Before the auction, prospective buyers will be given a brochure to review. The brochure explains the auction rules and requirements and also provides property information.

Auctions can be performed just about anywhere, but most of the time they are held on the property to be sold. The day of the auction is often the only time buyers will get the chance to inspect the property.

Typically, auctioned properties are sold as-is, with few or no contingencies. Buyers normally are required to make a down payment on the property in the form of a certified check, cashier's check or money order. The winning bidder usually has 30 to 60 days to finalize the transaction. If the deal doesn't close, the buyer's deposit can be forfeited.

So how much does it cost to sell property this way? Auctioneers say that the typical auction sale often costs the seller less than it would cost him or her to list the property with an agent. For more information, look in the Yellow Pages under Auctioneers for firms that specialize in real estate auctioning.

☞ **Money-$aving Tip #37** *When your house won't sell, consider lowering the price—within reason, of course. It's a good time to get an appraisal and then to lower the price to the appraised value—or perhaps even somewhat lower. The alternative may be months or even years on the market, ongoing mortgage payments, taxes and other costs to maintain the property.*

How *Your Agent Can Help*

Your real estate agent should provide you with a comprehensive plan for marketing your home—a plan that will define likely buyers, where to find them and how to reach them.

One of the first things your agent should do is place your home in the MLS—a marketing device that gives your property maximum exposure to the largest number of prospective buyers. Over the years, the MLS concept has grown from a strictly local sales tool into a powerful national and even international marketing system. In fact, many local MLS listings are now available on the Internet worldwide—increasing a home's exposure even more.

Advertising remains one of the most important components of the marketing process. In addition to newspaper and magazine ads, brokers and agents today use a variety of other proven advertising methods, including TV, radio, open houses, direct mail and the Internet.

A knowledgeable real estate agent will advertise your home expertly, show it skillfully and negotiate intelligently with buyers. Creative marketing has become the name of the game today. Your agent has the resources to provide innovative strategies targeted to the most likely prospects for your home.

Commonly Asked Questions

Q. What should I do about people who see the For Sale sign in my yard and then knock on the door asking to see the house?

A. If you're not selling the house yourself, refer them to the real estate agency whose phone number is on the sign. After all, that's one of the reasons you hired an agent in the first place—to avoid these kinds of situations.

Q. What is a Multiple Listing Service and why is it important in marketing my home?

A. The MLS is a marketing organization in which many brokers pool all of their listings and establish procedures for sharing commissions. Generally, Multiple Listing Services require that sellers sign an exclusive-agency or exclusive-right-to-sell listing with participating brokers in order to have access to the marketing pool.

The MLS is the backbone of the local real estate industry. It lists just about every home that is for sale in the area and is read religiously by every participating agent in every participating real estate office. So by putting your home in the MLS, you can be sure that it will get maximum exposure.

Q. What should a plan for marketing your house include?

A. A good marketing plan will include the following:
- A listing in the MLS database
- A detailed fact sheet highlighting the features of your home
- Suggestions on how to make your home more attractive to prospective buyers
- Ads in newspapers and magazines
- Signs
- Open house
- Other proven marketing techniques, such as direct mail, TV and radio advertising

CHAPTER 9

Analyzing and Negotiating Offers

The time will come when someone will hand you or your agent a written offer to buy your home. Should you accept the offer or should you make a counteroffer? Are there any contingencies? What should you do if you don't receive any offers? How does the negotiation process work? This chapter answers these questions and more.

The Agency Maze

When you sign a listing agreement, the agent agrees to do his or her best to sell your home at a mutually agreed-upon price. The agent is responsible to you and has only your interest in mind. For example, if you tell your agent that you are willing to accept $10,000 less than the asking price, he or she cannot ethically tell the buyer what you said. On the other hand, if the buyer tells your agent what he or she is willing to negotiate or what his or her top offer is, your agent is obligated to reveal this to you.

Until recently, most real estate agents involved in a given transaction worked for the seller, and thus were paid through commission on the sale of the home; usually there was no cost to the buyer.

Buyer's Agent

A relatively new concept in real estate is the agent who represents the buyer. A buyer's agent has only the buyer's interest in mind. Some buyer's agents are paid by the buyer in the form of a commission, a flat fee or an hourly rate. More likely, however, the buyer's agent will co-broker with the seller's agent; both will split the commission paid by the seller.

☞ **Money-$aving Tip #38** *Never tell a buyer's agent how low you'll go on your asking price if push comes to shove. If you confide that although your price is $150,000 you will go as low as $130,000, the buyer will soon know your intentions. That's because the buyer's agent is legally bound to secure the lowest price for the buyer.*

Dual Agent

An agent can represent both the buyer and the seller—in an arrangement called *dual agency*—but must have consent from both parties. A dual agent cannot represent the interests of one party to the exclusion or detriment of the other. And, he or she may not disclose one party's negotiating strategy or motivations to the other.

Because of confusion over representation, most states today require agents to reveal who they work for before an offer is made.

☞ **Money-$aving Tip #39** *A seller's agent is legally obligated to strive for the highest possible price for the property.*

The Real Estate Sales Contract

A real estate sales contract contains all the details of the agreement between a buyer and a seller for the purchase and sale of a home. The contract becomes legally binding once it is signed by both parties, and once acceptance has been communicated back to the offerer. For a sample contract, see Figure 9.1.

Parts of a Sales Contract

Although sales contracts will vary from state to state, the information generally required will include at least the following:

- The names of the buyer(s) and seller(s)
- The street address and legal description of the property
- The names of the brokers involved
- The purchase price, earnest money deposit, down payment and loan amount
- Conditions or contingencies that must be met
- The identification of any personal property included in the sale
- A time limit for the seller to accept the buyer's offer
- The responsibility for closing costs (recording fees, termite inspection, survey, title search, transfer fees, broker's commission, etc.)
- A provision for the proration of expenses at the time of closing—such as real estate taxes, water bills and hazard insurance

- Seller's escape clause (allowing the seller to keep the house on the market) if the buyer's offer has contingencies
- Disclosure of property conditions
- Any repairs the seller is required to make
- Disclosure of the broker's agency relationship
- A specified closing date
- The dated signatures of all parties

Fixtures versus Personal Property

When you sell a house, it is understood that you are also selling those parts of the house, called *fixtures,* that are permanently attached or built in and are intended to be a part of the home. Common fixtures include built-in dishwashers, a central air-conditioning system, chandeliers and plumbing. *Personal property,* on the other hand, refers to tangible items not permanently attached and not intended to go with the property; the dining-room table and chairs, the washer and dryer out in the garage and the countertop microwave oven in the kitchen are examples of personal property.

Generally speaking, an item remains personal property if it can be removed without serious injury either to the house or to the item itself. For example, a window air conditioner ordinarily would be considered personal property, but if a hole were cut in a wall expressly for the installation of the air conditioner, the unit would probably be considered a fixture and remain with the property.

The best way to avoid disputes is to stipulate in the contract which items stay and which items go. In the absence of such an agreement, however, legal action ultimately might decide the issue. If litigation is necessary because it is unclear whether an item is a fixture or personal property, the courts generally will favor the buyer over the seller.

FIGURE 9.1 Sample Real Estate Sales Contract

REALTOR®

EQUAL HOUSING OPPORTUNITY

PURCHASE AND SALE CONTRACT FOR RESIDENTIAL PROPERTY

Plain English Form published by and only for use of members of the Greater Rochester Association of Realtors, Inc. and the Monroe County Bar Association.

COMMISSIONS OR FEES FOR THE REAL ESTATE SERVICES TO BE PROVIDED ARE NEGOTIABLE BETWEEN REALTOR AND CLIENT.

When Signed, This Document Becomes A Binding Contract. Buyer or Seller May Wish To Consult Their Own Attorney.

TO: ______________________________ (Seller) FROM: ______________________________ (Buyer)

OFFER TO PURCHASE

Buyer offers to purchase the property described below from Seller on the following terms:

1. PROPERTY DESCRIPTION.

Property known as No. ______________________ in the (Town) (City) (Village) of ______________________, State of New York, also known as Tax No. ______________________ including all buildings and any other improvements and all rights which the Seller has in or with the property.

Approximate Lot Size: ______________________. (Check if applicable) [ ] As described in more detail in the attached description.

Description of Buildings on Property: ______________________

2. OTHER ITEMS INCLUDED IN PURCHASE. The following items, if any, now in or on the property are included in this purchase and sale. All heating, plumbing, septic and private water systems, lighting fixtures, flowers, shrubs, trees, window shades and blinds, curtain and traverse rods, storm windows, storm doors, screens, awnings, TV antennae, water softeners, sump pumps, window boxes, mail box, tool shed, fences, underground pet containment fencing with control devices, wall-to-wall carpeting and runners, exhaust fans, hoods, garbage disposal, electric garage door opener and remote control devices, intercom equipment, humidifier, security systems, smoke detectors, all fireplace screens and enclosures, swimming pool and all related equipment and accessories, and the following, if built-in: cabinets, mirrors, stoves, ovens, dishwashers, trash compactors, shelving and air conditioning (except window units). Buyer agrees to accept these items in their present conditions. Other items to be included in the purchase and sale are:

____

[ ] Seller represents to the best of Seller's knowledge that any heating, plumbing, air conditioning, electrical systems and included appliances are presently in good working order, except for

____

Items not included are: ______________________

Seller represents that he has good title to all of the above items to be transferred to Buyer, and will deliver a Bill of Sale for the same at closing.

3. PRICE: AMOUNT AND HOW IT WILL BE PAID: The purchase price is ______________________ Dollars $ ______________, Buyer shall receive credit at closing for any deposit made hereunder. The balance of the purchase price shall be paid as follows: (Check and complete applicable provisions.)

[ ] (a) Seller agrees to pay a loan fee of ________% of the mortgage amount.

[ ] (b) All in cash, or certified check at closing.

[ ] (c) By Buyer assuming and agreeing to pay according to its terms, the principal balance of the mortgage in the approximate amount of $ ______________ held by ______________________, provided that the mortgage is assumable without the holder's approval. Buyer understands that the mortgage bears interest at the rate of ________% per year and the monthly payments are $ ______________ which includes principal, interest, taxes and insurance (strike out any item not included in payment), with the last payment due on approximately ______________ 19/20________. Buyer agrees to pay the balance of the purchase price over the amount of the assumed mortgage in cash or certified check at closing. Buyer understands that principal balance may be lower at time of closing because of monthly payments made after this contract is signed. If the mortgage to be assumed provides for graduated or balloon payments, then a copy of the original bond and mortgage shall be furnished to Buyer's attorney for approval within ten days after acceptance of this offer.

[ ] (d) By Buyer delivering a purchase money bond and mortgage to Seller at closing. This purchase money bond and mortgage shall be in the amount of $______________, shall be amortized over a term of ________ years and all due and payable in ________ years from the date of closing, shall bear interest at the rate of ________% per year, and shall be paid in monthly installments of $______________, including principal and interest. The mortgage shall contain the statutory clauses as to payment, insurance, acceleration on default of thirty days, taxes, assessments, and water rates and also shall provide for late charges of 2% of any monthly payment which is not paid within 15 days after it is due and for recovery of reasonable attorney's fees if the mortgage is foreclosed.

The mortgage shall allow Buyer to prepay all or part of the mortgage without penalty at any time but shall also provide that the mortgage be paid in full if Buyer sells the property, unless Seller consents in writing to assumption of the mortgage debt. The balance of the purchase price will be paid at closing in cash, or certified check.

4. CONTINGENCIES. Buyer makes this offer subject to the following contingencies. If any of these contingencies is not satisfied by the dates specified, then either Buyer or Seller may cancel this contract by written notice to the other. (Check and complete applicable provisions.)

[ ] (a) **Mortgage Contingency.** This offer subject to Buyer obtaining and accepting a ______________ mortgage loan commitment in an amount not to exceed ______________ at an interest rate not to exceed ________%, for a term of ________ years. Buyer shall immediately apply for this loan and shall have until ______________ to obtain and accept a written mortgage commitment. The conditions of any such mortgage commitment shall not be deemed contingencies of this contract but shall be the sole responsibility of Buyer. If the loan commitment requires repairs, replacements, or improvements to be made or painting to be done, before closing, then Seller shall do the work and install the materials and improvements needed or have the same done, at Seller's expense. However, if the cost of doing so exceeds $______________, Seller shall not be obligated to have such work done, and Buyer will be allowed either to receive credit at closing for the amount recited above and incur any necessary expenses to comply with the loan commitment requirements, or to cancel this contract by written notice to Seller, and any deposit shall be returned to Buyer. Issuance and acceptance by the Buyer of a written mortgage commitment shall be deemed a waiver and satisfaction of this contingency.

[ ] (b) **Mortgage Assumption Contingency.** This offer is subject to Buyer obtaining permission to assume the existing mortgage loan balance referred to above in (3c) by ________ 19______. If the mortgage holder requires that the interest rate be increased for such approval to be given, Buyer agrees to assume the mortgage at such rate as long as it does not exceed ______% at the time of the commitment. [ ]Buyer agrees to obtain a release of Seller's liability and to pay any assumption or release of liability fees.

[ ] (c) **Sale Contract Contingency.** This offer is subject to Buyer obtaining a contract for the sale of Buyer's property located at ______________ no later than ______________, 199______. Unless and until Buyer has removed this sale contingency in writing, if Seller receives another acceptable purchase offer, Seller may notify Buyer in writing that Seller wants to accept the other offer and Buyer will then have ______________ days to remove this sale contingency by written notice to the Seller. If Buyer does not remove this sale contingency after receiving notice from Seller, Buyer's rights under this contract shall end, and Seller shall be free to accept the other purchase offer and Buyer's deposit shall be returned. Buyer may not remove this sale contingency if Buyer's mortgage loan commitment requires the sale and/or transfer of this property as a condition of the mortgage loan funding, unless Buyer has a contract for the sale of this property which is not then subject to any unsatisfied contingencies.

[ ] (d) **Transfer of Title Contingency.** This offer is contingent upon the transfer of title to Buyer's property located at ______________ no later than ______________, 199______. [ ] Buyer represents that Buyer has entered into a contract for sale of Buyer's property which is now subject to the following contingencies: [ ] None; [ ] Mortgage; [ ] Assumption of Mortgage; [ ] Sale of Property; [ ] Transfer of Title; [ ] Attorney Approval; and/or [ ] Other______________. Unless and until Buyer has obtained a contract for sale of Buyer's property which is not subject to any unsatisfied contingencies, and has so notified the Seller in writing, if Seller receives another acceptable purchase offer, Seller may notify Buyer in writing that Seller wants to accept the other offer and Buyer will then have ______________ days to remove this transfer of title contingency by written notice to the Seller. If Buyer does not remove this transfer of title contingency after receiving notice from Seller, Buyer's rights under this contract shall end, and Seller shall be free to accept the other purchase offer and Buyer's deposit shall be returned. Buyer may not remove this transfer of title contingency if Buyer's mortgage loan commitment requires the sale and transfer of this property as a condition of the mortgage loan funding, unless Buyer has a contract for sale of this property which is not then subject to any unsatisfied contingencies.

[ ] (e) **Attorney Approval.** This contract is subject to the written approval of attorneys for Buyer and Seller within ______________ days from date of acceptance (the "Approval Period"). If either attorney makes written objection to the contract within the Approval Period, and such objection is not cured by written approval by both attorneys and all of the parties within the Approval Period, then either Buyer or Seller may cancel this contract by written notice to the other and any deposit shall be returned to the Buyer.

[ ] (f) **Waiver of Attorney Approval.** This offer is not subject to the Buyer's attorney approval.

[ ] (g) **Other Contingencies.** ______________________

5. Closing Date and Place. Transfer of title shall take place at the ______________ County Clerk's Office or at the offices of Buyer's lender on or before ______________________, 19________.

6. Buyer's Possession of Property.

[ ] Buyer shall have possession of the property on the day of closing, in broom clean condition, with all keys to the property delivered to Buyer at closing.

[ ] Seller shall have the right to retain possession for______________ days after closing at the cost of $______________ per day, plus utilities. At possession, the property shall be broom clean and all keys shall be delivered to Buyer.

7. Title Documents. Seller shall provide the following documents in connection with the sale:

A. Deed. Seller will deliver to Buyer at closing a properly signed and notarized Warranty Deed with lien covenant (or Executor's Deed, Administrator's Deed or Trustee's Deed, if Seller holds title as such).

GRAR 3/94 **B. Abstract, Bankruptcy and Tax Searches, and Instrument Survey Map.** Seller will furnish and pay for and deliver to Buyer or Buyer's attorney at least 15 days prior to the date of closing, fully guaranteed tax, title and United States Court Searches dated or redated after the date of this contract with a local tax certificate for Village, or City taxes, if any, and an instrument survey map dated or redated after the date of this contract. Seller will pay for the map or redated map and for continuing such searches to and including the day of closing. Any survey map shall be prepared or redated and certified to meet the standards and requirements of Buyer's mortgage lender and of the Monroe County Bar Association.

FIGURE 9.1 Sample Real Estate Sales Contract (Continued)

8. Marketability of Title. The deed and other documents delivered by Seller shall be sufficient to convey good marketable title in fee simple, to the property free and clear of all liens and encumbrances. However, Buyer agrees to accept title to the property subject to restrictive covenants of record common to the tract or subdivision of which the property is a part, provided these restrictions have not been violated, or if they have been violated, that the time for anyone to complain of the violations has expired. Buyer also agrees to accept title to the property subject to public utility easements along lot lines as long as those easements do not interfere with any buildings now on the property or with any improvements Buyer may construct in compliance with all present restrictive covenants of record and zoning and building codes applicable to the Property. Seller agrees to furnish a smoke alarm affidavit at closing and to cooperate in executing any documents required by federal or state laws for transfer of title to residential property.

9. Objections to Title. If Buyer raises a valid written objection to Seller's title which means that the title to the property is unmarketable, Seller may cancel this contract by giving prompt written notice of cancellation to Buyer. Buyer's deposit shall be returned immediately, and if Buyer makes a written request for it, Seller shall reimburse Buyer for the reasonable cost of having the title examined. However, if Seller gives notice within 5 days that Seller will cure the problem prior to the closing date, or if the title objection is insurable and Buyer is willing to accept insurable title, then this contract shall continue in force until the closing date, subject to the Seller performing as promised and/or providing insurable title at Seller's expense. If Seller fails to cure the problem within such time, Buyer will not be obligated to purchase the property and Buyer's deposit shall be returned together with reimbursement for the reasonable cost of having the title examined.

10. Recording Costs, Mortgage Tax, Transfer Tax and Closing Adjustments. Seller will pay the real property transfer tax and special additional mortgage recording tax, if applicable. Buyer will pay mortgage assumption charges, if any, and will pay for recording the deed and the mortgage, and for mortgage tax. The following, as applicable, will be prorated and adjusted between Seller and Buyer as of the date of closing: current taxes computed on a fiscal year basis, excluding any delinquent items, interest and penalties; rent payments; fuel oil on the premises; water charges; pure water charges; sewer charges; mortgage interest; current common charges or assessments; prepaid F.H.A. Mortgage Insurance Premium (M.I.P.) of approximately $ _____ with the exact amount to be calculated at closing in accordance with F.H.A. formulae. Any F.H.A. insurance premium which is not prepaid, but rather paid monthly, shall be adjusted at closing. If there is a water meter at the property, Seller shall furnish an actual reading to a date not more than thirty (30) days before the closing date set forth in this contract. At closing the water charges and any sewer rent shall be apportioned on the basis of such actual reading.

11. Zoning. Seller represents that the property is in full compliance with all zoning or building ordinances for use as a _____. If applicable laws require it, the Seller will furnish at or before closing, a Certificate of Occupancy for the property, dated within ninety (90) days of the closing, with Seller completing the work and installing the materials and improvements needed to obtain Certificate of Occupancy. However, if the cost of obtaining a Certificate of Occupancy exceeds $ _____, Seller shall not be obligated to have such work done, and Buyer will be allowed either to receive credit at closing for the amount recited above, and incur the necessary expenses to obtain the Certificate of Occupancy, or to cancel this contract by written notice to Seller, and any deposit shall be returned to Buyer.

12. Risk of Loss. Risk of loss or damage to the property by fire or other casualty until transfer of title shall be assumed by the Seller. If damage to the property by fire or such other casualty occurs prior to transfer, Buyer may cancel this contract without any further liability to Seller and Buyer's deposit is to be returned. If Buyer does not cancel but elects to close, then Seller shall transfer to Buyer any insurance proceeds, or Seller's claim to insurance proceeds payable for such damage.

13. Condition of Property. Buyer agrees to purchase the property "as is" except as provided in paragraph 2, subject to reasonable use, wear, tear, and natural deterioration between now and the time of closing. However, this paragraph is not called for when furnishing a Certificate of Occupancy as called for in paragraph 11, if applicable. Buyer shall have the right, after reasonable notice to Seller, to inspect the property within 48 hours before the time of closing.

14. Services. Seller represents that property is serviced by: _____ Public Water, _____ Public Sewers, _____ Septic System, _____ Private Well.

15. Deposit to Listing Broker. Buyer (has deposited) (will deposit upon acceptance) $ _____ in the form of a _____ with _____ (Escrow Agent) at _____ (bank), which deposit is to become part of the purchase price or returned if not accepted or if Buyer's contract thereafter fails to close for any reason not the fault of the Buyer. If Buyer fails to complete Buyer's part of this contract, Seller is allowed to retain the deposit to be applied to Seller's damages, and may also pursue other legal rights Seller has against the Buyer, including a lawsuit for any real estate brokerage commission paid by the Seller.

16. Real Estate Broker.
[ ] The parties agree that _____ brought about this purchase and sale.
[ ] It is understood and agreed by both Buyer and Seller that no broker secured this contract.

17. Life of Offer. This offer shall expire on _____, 19___, at _____ m.

18. Responsibility of Persons Under This Contract; Assignability. If more than one person signs this contract as Buyer, each person and any party who takes over that person's legal position will be responsible for keeping the promises made by Buyer in this contract. If more than one person signs this contract as Seller, each person or any party who takes over that person's legal position, will be fully responsible for keeping the promises made by Seller. However, this contract is personal to the parties and may not be assigned by either without the other's consent.

19. Entire Contract. This contract when signed by both Buyer and Seller will be the record of the complete agreement between the Buyer and Seller concerning the purchase and sale of the property. No verbal agreements or promises will be binding.

20. Notices. All notices under this contract shall be deemed delivered upon receipt. Any notices relating to this contract may be given by the attorneys for the parties.

21. Addenda. The following Addenda are incorporated into this contract:
[ ] All Parties Agreement   [ ] Services   [ ] Engineer's Inspection   [ ] Mediation   [ ] Electric Availability   [ ] Utility Surcharge   [ ] Lead Warning   [ ] Other: _____

Dated: _____   BUYER _____

Witness: _____   BUYER _____

[ ] ACCEPTANCE OF OFFER BY SELLER   [ ] COUNTER OFFER BY SELLER
Seller certifies that Seller owns the property and has the power to sell the property. Seller accepts the offer and agrees to sell on the terms and conditions above set forth.
[ ] Waiver of Seller's attorney approval. This offer is not subject to Seller's attorney approval.

Dated: _____   SELLER _____

Witness: _____   SELLER _____

ADMINISTRATIVE INFORMATION

Buyer: _____

Social Security Number: _____

Address: _____

_____ Zip: _____

Phone: (H) _____ (B) _____

Attorney: _____

Address: _____

Phone: (B) _____ (FAX) _____

Selling Broker: _____

Address: _____

Phone: _____ Broker Code: _____

Selling Agent: _____ Phone: (H) _____

Selling Agent I.D. # _____ FAX _____

Seller: _____

Social Security Number: _____

GRAR MLS # _____

Address: _____

_____ Zip: _____

Phone: (H) _____ (B) _____

Attorney: _____

Address: _____

Phone: (B) _____ (FAX) _____

Listing Broker: _____

Address: _____

Phone: _____ Broker Code: _____

Listing Agent: _____ Phone: (H) _____

Listing Agent I.D. # _____ FAX _____

☞ **Money-$aving Tip #40** *Don't let nickels and dimes botch the deal. Picture this: You've just about sold your house. The buyer thinks the property is perfect and the price is right. But hold on: The buyer is rather fond of the light fixture in the dining room and insists that it stays. You refuse to part with it. Never mind that the light fixture is worth about $150, while the house was appraised at $200,000. The deal is off!*

☞ **Money-$aving Tip #41** *Be sure to spell out in the contract all personal items about which there may be disputes as to whether they stay with the property.*

The Offer

When a prospective buyer is ready to make an offer on your home, the agent for the buyer will draw up a sales contract and present it to your agent. The offer should specify a date by which you must decide whether to accept it, reject it or make a counteroffer to it. Usually, you have one or two days to consider the offer. During this period, the ball is in your court; now you have a chance to make a deal with the buyer. Talk it over with your agent before you decide how to respond. The rest of this chapter focuses on some of the issues you'll want to weigh carefully in judging offers that you receive.

☞ **Money-$aving Tip #42** *Nothing you and the buyer say to each other is binding unless it's contained in a written contract. So never discuss an oral offer on your house—you might reveal some of your selling strategy to the buyer.*

Price

In evaluating offers, start with the premise that you aren't going to get everything you want. Take price, for starters. Unless you are in a hot market, the buyer most likely will offer less than your asking price. But is the offer reasonably close to the price you want? Most buyers and sellers will negotiate on price, with both sides "giving" a little until an agreement is reached.

☞ **Money-$aving Tip #43** *Find out all you can about the prospective buyer's situation to help you in price negotiations.*

Earnest Money Deposit

When a buyer makes an offer, it will include an *earnest money deposit*—that is, money, usually in the form of a check, that shows the buyer is serious about purchasing the home. The deposit should be large enough to discourage the buyer from defaulting, compensate the seller for taking the property off the market and cover any expenses the seller might incur if the buyer does default. An offer with no earnest money, however, is still valid.

Earnest money is held in a special escrow account. If the offer is accepted, the earnest money will be included as part of the buyer's down payment. If the offer is not accepted, the earnest money will be given back to the buyer. In limited circumstances (i.e., the buyer backs out for no reason), he or she forfeits the full amount. Frequently, the buyer backs out *and* receives the earnest money back.

Down Payment

Look at the down payment the buyer is offering. Is it sufficient? Ask your agent whether the buyer is qualified to purchase the home. Remember, the best offer in the world is worthless if the buyer can't follow through.

What the Offer Is Really Worth

How much money will you net from the offer? This is a critical question that can be used to analyze the offer. For example, assume this scenario:

- Your asking price is $190,000, which is $6,000 higher than market value.
- There is a mortgage payoff of $35,000.
- The prospective buyer offers $180,000.
- The contract calls for you to replace the roof at a cost of $6,000 and pay $4,000 of the buyer's closing costs.
- Broker's commission is $12,600.
- Other selling expenses, $5,000.

When you receive an offer, your agent should prepare a *net proceeds statement* to give you a rough estimate of what you can expect to net at closing. Using the information above, your net proceeds can be found as follows:

Sales price		$180,000
Less:		
Mortgage payoff	$35,000	
Cost of new roof	6,000	
Buyer's closing costs	4,000	
Commission	12,000	
Other seller expenses	5,000	
Total costs		62,000
Net proceeds		$118,000

Knowing your bottom line can help you evaluate any offers you receive. It may be that $118,000 is acceptable to you. The important point is that within the agreement are costs that make the proposed deal worth considerably less than the offering price of $180,000.

But if the bottom line means you can't buy your next home, or you just want your profit to be higher, you can either say no to the deal or you can make a counteroffer with modifications. Keep in mind, however, that it's ultimately the marketplace that determines what the home is worth.

Contingencies

An offer to purchase your house may contain contingencies that must be satisfied before the sales contract becomes fully enforceable. As you look through the contingencies, ask yourself whether they are reasonable.

The most common one is a mortgage contingency, which protects the buyer's earnest money until a lender has committed the mortgage loan funds. A financing contingency is acceptable as long as the terms of the loan and the time-frame are reasonable.

A common practice in some areas is to make a sales contract contingent on the buyer obtaining professional inspections of the property being purchased. Inspections may include those for termites, structural and electro-mechanical systems and radon or other toxic materials. Or a buyer may make the sales contract contingent on the sale of his or her current home. This protects the buyer from being legally bound to the purchase before the buyer's existing home is sold. In such a case, the seller may insist on some protection (often called an *escape clause*) in case the buyer's house doesn't sell. For example, the seller may want to keep the house on the market and continue to solicit additional buyers, giving the original buyer the right of first refusal. This means that if the seller receives another offer during the contingency period, the original buyer retains the right to either eliminate the contingency or to void the contract.

Time Limits

If you accept an offer with contingencies, you're effectively taking the house off the market with no guarantee that the sale will go through. So it is customary to specify time limits in the sales contract for all contingencies.

Other dates of importance are the closing date and the date on which the seller must give possession to the buyer. Be sure these dates are acceptable.

The Art of Negotiation

There are no rules to guide negotiations. Each property transfer is its own unique story. Successful agents find out all they can about the buyers and sellers and the property without getting emotionally involved. They establish what both parties are trying to accomplish, anticipate needs, determine acceptable minimum and maximum positions and create options and alternatives in case negotiations break down. A good agent can save a deal by making both parties feel like winners. Negotiation is an art, but it is also a business. Everyone should leave the negotiating table with a feeling of victory.

☞ **Money-Saving Tip #44** *Make up your mind in advance—and keep it to yourself—about the least amount of money you would accept for your house if you had to.*

Here are some tried-and-tested guidelines that are crucial to the negotiating process:

- Establish what is important and what is minor. If you need to, offer items that are less significant to you, such as closing or move-in dates, instead of items that are critical to you, such as price.
- Begin negotiations by asking for more than you expect to receive, but not so much more that you insult or discourage the other party.
- Listen carefully to the prospective buyer's objections and arguments. Try to determine what it is he or she really wants.
- Keep the buyer aware of all the property benefits.

- Never humiliate those with whom you are negotiating or back them into a corner.
- Don't be too anxious to make concessions. A sophisticated buyer will use this to his or her advantage during the negotiations.
- Balance the table through give and take. Ensure that everyone gives up something to get something. Let everyone leave the table feeling they have "won."
- Recognize the risks of negotiating. If you reject an offer from a buyer, or make a counteroffer, the original offer is dead unless the buyer chooses to revive it.
- Always leave the door open and have patience enough to play the waiting game.

Making a Counteroffer

After evaluating an offer, you have three options:

- Accept it
- Reject it
- Make a counteroffer

In weighing an offer, you need to consider what is important to you and what is not. In the counteroffer, you may want to increase the price or change the terms. Be sure to spell out all the modifications you want to make. Your agent will relay any counteroffers back to the agent for the buyer who will then relay the offer to the buyers. The buyers can accept the offer or can make another offer, in which case the process starts over.

Often, several offers go back and forth until an offer is accepted or one party decides to end negotiations.

Remember: Any time you make a counteroffer, you give the prospective buyer the opportunity to walk away. Don't dicker over trivial things. Be sure the changes you want to make are worth the risk.

What to Do If You Don't Get Any Serious Offers

If you aren't getting any offers on your home, don't hit the panic button just yet. Answer these questions to see whether you can pinpoint the problem:

- Have you given your agent enough time to sell your home? The process of selling a home, even in the best of circumstances, is likely to take several months.
- Has the house had enough exposure? Review your agent's marketing plan.
- Take a look at market conditions. Is the market soft or is it reviving? Are mortgage interest rates going down, going up or remaining the same? What about house prices? Is the type of house you're selling plentiful or scarce?
- Is your house in tip-top shape? Often, the condition of the home plays a major role in the overall selling equation.
- Is your house priced fairly for today's residential real estate market? Check it out. It's hard to sell a home for a price that is not reasonably consistent with the neighborhood.

If fine-tuning the home's condition, marketing plan and price doesn't soon reverse the situation, you may have to entice buyers by offering them something extra. For example, you may agree to pay some of the closing costs. Or you may want to offer a redecorating allowance. Incentives such as these are covered in Chapter 8.

Accepting an Offer

Once the seller and buyer agree to the original offer or to a later counteroffer exactly as it was made and both parties sign the contract, the offer has been accepted. The broker then must advise the buyer of the seller's acceptance and deliver a duplicate original of the contract to each party. At this point, for all practical purposes, you've sold your house. (Technically, a house is not sold until title passes.) Now you can prepare for the final step—the closing.

How Your Agent Can Help

The sales contract is the most important document you will sign. It will describe in precise legal terms how much you are being paid, when you will be paid and what you are selling. The contract also includes the legal obligations you and the buyer have regarding the sale of the house. Ask your real estate broker or agent to review the sales contract in detail with you to be sure it reflects the deal you want.

While it's your decision to accept or reject an offer or present a counteroffer, your agent can be of great help to you during the negotiating process. In fact, negotiation is one of the valuable skills an agent uses to bring opposing parties to mutually satisfactory settlements.

Commonly Asked Questions

Q. Are oral offers legally binding?

A. No. A sales contract or offer to purchase—whatever the agreement is called in your area—must be in writing to be legally enforceable.

Q. How much earnest money is required to make a contract binding?

A. None. An earnest money deposit is not a legal requirement. It can, however, be a good indicator of how serious a person is about wanting to buy—especially if the amount is substantial.

Q. How can I find out about a prospective buyer's finances?

A. One of the things your agent will do is to *qualify* the buyer by analyzing the buyer's stated income, assets, debts, and available cash to determine whether the buyer is financially capable of buying your home.

Q. When can a buyer's offer be withdrawn?

A. An offer can be withdrawn at any time prior to the seller's acceptance. Or, if the seller makes any changes, the original offer is dead and the buyer is free of any obligation.

Q. What are contingencies?

A. They are provisions in a sales contract that require certain acts to be done or certain events to occur before the contract becomes binding. For example, a buyer may make his or her offer subject to a satisfactory home inspection or subject to a loan being approved for $80,000 with an interest rate no higher than 9 percent. However, once signed, even with contingencies, a contract is binding. Keep in mind that until all contingencies are satisfied, the contract could fail to close with no legal ramifications.

CHAPTER 10

What You Should Know about Your Buyer's Financing

As a seller, you may feel that dealing with lenders is the buyer's problem, not yours—and that's basically true. But while you are not looking for a loan, it's in your best interest to understand the lending system for several reasons. For example, if a prospective buyer makes an offer but can't finance the deal down the road, you continue to pay the mortgage and other expenses each month while the sale is delayed. Or, what happens if you receive two offers that are pretty much similar? Which one do you choose? Knowing a little about how the lending system works can help you make your choice.

Besides, you might be a seller now, but after the deal is done you're likely to become a buyer. And, because your next house will probably be financed, learning everything you can about the mortgage game and the choices available to you will ultimately help you when it's your turn to buy.

Mortgage Payment Plans

A mortgage is a claim that a lender receives on a property as security for the loan it makes to a homebuyer. Repayment of a mortgage requires payment of both *principal* (the amount borrowed) and *interest* (the charge for the borrowing).

Today, a veritable smorgasbord of loans, with terms from 15 to 40 years, is available to satisfy the needs of both lender and borrower. The interest rate can be *fixed* (the same for the life of the loan) or *adjustable* (based on the interest rates of U.S. Treasury bills or other established indices).

Most mortgage loans are *amortized loans.* Regular payments are made over a term of 15 to 30 years, and each payment is applied first to the interest owed with the balance being applied to the principal amount. At the end of the term, the full amount of the principal and all interest due will be reduced to zero. Most amortized mortgage loans are paid in monthly installments.

Types of Mortgages

Fully amortized fixed-rate mortgage. This is the most popular home financing method, requiring regular payments of both principal and interest so that the loan is fully paid off at the end of the loan term.

Adjustable-rate mortgage (ARM). With an ARM, individual payments can rise or fall as the interest rate rises or falls in step with the index used. Most ARMs feature an interest rate that is below market for the first year, after which the rate most likely will go up.

The typical ARM has two types of interest rate caps:

1. A *lifetime cap,* which limits the amount the rate can increase over the life of the loan

2. A *periodic cap,* which limits the amount the rate can increase or decrease within one adjustment period

Most ARMs allow a maximum movement of two percentage points a year and six percentage points over the life of the loan.

Lenders may offer a *conversion option,* which allows you to convert from an adjustable-rate to a fixed-rate loan at certain intervals during the loan. The option will stipulate the terms and conditions for the conversion.

Loan Terms

Loans come in a variety of lengths, but the most common offer a 30-year or a 15-year term. The longer the loan period, the smaller the monthly principal and interest payment.

The 30-year fixed-rate mortgage is still the standard and is designed especially for buyers who need a smaller monthly payment to balance their budgets and who expect to stay in their homes for a long time. In the early years of a mortgage, most of the payment is for interest. On a 30-year loan at 7.5 percent interest, the principal payment does not exceed the interest payment until year 21. If this loan were for $100,000, you would pay more than $151,700 in interest over 30 years. Because the borrower pays more interest than principal for the first 20 years, the tax deduction is substantial.

Although a 15-year mortgage means higher monthly payments than an equivalent 30-year mortgage, you pay considerably less in interest over the life of the loan. For example, on a $100,000 loan at 7.5 percent interest you would pay only about $66,800 in interest over 15 years, as opposed to more than $151,700 in interest over a 30-year term—a difference of nearly $85,000.

Conventional Loans

Conventional mortgage loans are secured from a bank or other lending institution with no government agency insuring or guaranteeing the loan. In the mortgage arrangement, the borrower uses the property as collateral for the loan made by the lender. The lender assumes full risk of a default by the borrower. Some states will issue a deed of trust instead of a mortgage, where a third party holds the deed to the property until the loan is repaid.

At this writing, conventional loans are available for amounts up to $207,000 (not to be confused with "jumbo loans," which can exceed the conventional limit) and usually require at least a 20 percent down payment. The security for the loan is provided solely by the mortgage. The payment of the debt rests on the borrower's ability to pay. A lender's decision to make a conventional loan is usually dependent on the following:

- The credit and income position of the borrower
- The value of the property being used to secure the debt

The lender relies primarily on its appraisal of the property and information from credit reports that indicate the reliability of the prospective borrower.

Buyers who qualify for conventional financing, but who can't handle the high down payment requirement, can put down significantly less than 20 percent by purchasing *private mortgage insurance* (PMI). This insurance protects the lender in case the buyer defaults on the loan and may be paid as part of the monthly mortgage payment. By using PMI, the buyer may be able to get a fixed-rate or adjustable-rate mortgage by putting as little as 5 percent down.

Loan-to-Value Ratio

You may have heard lenders use the term *loan-to-value ratio* or *LTV* ratio. An LTV ratio is simply the relationship between the amount of money borrowed and the appraised value or purchase price of the property—whichever is less. For example, an $80,000 loan on property valued at $100,000 would represent an 80 percent LTV ratio. So an 80 percent LTV loan requires a down payment of 20 percent. With a 5 percent down payment, the buyer has a 95 percent LTV ratio.

As you can see, the lower the LTV ratio, the higher the down payment required of the borrower. For the lender, the higher down payment means a more secure, lower-risk loan. Conventional loans are viewed as the most secure loans because the LTV ratio is lowest—usually 80 percent of the value of the property or lower; that is, the borrower makes a down payment of 20 percent or more.

Government-Backed Loans

For most people, the down payment is the biggest stumbling block they face on the road to home ownership. To make home ownership more affordable, the government decided to provide home loans that require very low and sometimes no down payments. The government doesn't actually lend money to the homebuyer. Banks or other lending institutions still make the loans, but the government insures, or guarantees, them, protecting the lender against borrower default. The two most common types of government-insured loans are FHA (Federal Housing Administration) and VA (Department of Veterans Affairs) loans.

FHA Loans

The common term *FHA loan* refers to a loan that is not made by the Federal Housing Administration but *insured* by it. The actual loans are made by approved FHA lending institutions. As with private mortgage insurance, the FHA insures the lender against loss from a borrower's default.

Just about anyone can apply for an FHA-insured mortgage through FHA-approved banks and other lending institutions—provided the loan amount doesn't exceed the maximum allowed by law. At this writing, the maximum FHA loan is $152,362 for a single-family residence in high-cost urban areas; in low-cost areas, it is $85,000 or less.

> **Note:** In Alaska, Hawaii and Guam, maximum FHA loan amounts are higher than in the continental United States.

FHA loans are desirable from a prospective buyer's standpoint because of the low down payment requirements. With FHA financing, the down payment required is a minimum of 3 percent on the first $25,000 borrowed and 5 percent on the rest. The lower down payment, of course, helps buyers who don't have a lot of up-front cash. Historically, the interest rate on FHA-insured mortgages is lower than the rates available for conventional loans.

VA Loans

VA financing is available either to active military personnel or to veterans, and often requires no down payment. The interest rate is generally less than those for conventional loans.

At this time, the maximum limit on a VA loan is over $200,000. As with FHA loans, the VA does not actually loan homebuyers money; rather the money comes from a VA-approved lending institution. The VA partially guarantees loans made by these institutions. The lender would receive the amount of the guarantee from the VA if a foreclosure sale did not bring enough to cover the outstanding loan balance. VA financing is available to active military personnel and veterans.

Assumable Mortgages

An *assumable mortgage* is one that passes to the new owner when a property is sold. An assumable mortgage with a below-market interest rate can be an added attraction when you sell your home; the prospective buyer can save a lot of money on interest and at the same time, save the costs of applying for a new loan. As a seller, you or your agent should check to see if you have such a mortgage.

FHA loans made before December 1, 1986, and VA loans made before March 1, 1988, are completely assumable. This means that the buyer does not have to be qualified by a lender to assume the loan. Closing costs are minimal, interest rates will remain the same, and the transaction can be closed and settled quickly.

Newer FHA and VA loans, however, are classified as "assumable with the lender's approval." To take over the newer FHA mortgages, the next borrower must be qualified by a lender and meet all FHA guidelines. Many ARMs also fall into this group—that is, they can be assumed with the lender's approval.

Conventional loans—those not backed by the FHA or VA—usually are not assumable. That is, the loan must be paid off when the property is sold.

If a mortgage is not assumable, most lenders will include a *due-on-sale clause* (also called an *alienation clause*) in the mortgage. This clause requires the borrower to repay the outstanding balance when the property is sold. The lender may allow the mortgage to be assumed, but only after adjusting the interest rate to reflect current market conditions.

Debt-to-Income Ratio

Lenders look at how much of the borrower's household income will be used to pay for mortgage principal, mortgage interest, property taxes and property insurance—what lenders call *PITI*. Lenders then look at how much of the borrower's income will be used to pay total debts, which include PITI, car payments, credit cards and other fixed expenses.

Most lenders want debt-to-income ratios of 28 and 36 for conventional loans, meaning that no more than 28 percent of the borrower's gross income will go to PITI, and no more than 36 percent of the borrower's gross income will go toward total debts including PITI.

The FHA program has more liberal qualification standards than conventional financing. Instead of 28/36 debt-to-income ratios, an FHA borrower can qualify with ratios of 29 and 41.

The VA uses one ratio—income to total debts. For VA loans, the percentage of total debt to income cannot exceed 41 percent. If it does, offsetting factors—an excellent credit history, long-term employment, little or no increase in housing costs and military benefits—would have to be considered before the loan could be approved. Contact your FHA representative for more details.

☞ **Money-$aving Tip #45** *If your mortgage has an assumable clause, check to see whether you can use the interest rate and other terms as a selling point. In some cases, you may be able to offer the buyer a bargain mortgage. For example, if the going interest rate is 9 percent and you have an assumable mortgage at 7 percent, your loan should be worth something to the buyer.*

Caution: If your mortgage has an assumable clause, be sure you're not liable if the buyer defaults. You can release yourself from all liability by requiring that the buyer be qualified by the lender. Your broker or attorney can tell you whether you run any risks.

Points

In real estate jargon, one *point* equals 1 percent of the total loan amount. If you buy a house for $125,000 and borrow $100,000, one point would equal $1,000, not $1,250; two points would equal $2,000.

Buyers often pay points to lending institutions to get a better interest rate on a mortgage. For example, a lender may offer a choice of two 30-year, fixed-rate mortgages: the first at 8.5 percent with zero points, and the second at 8 percent with two points. If the loan is for $100,000, those two points will cost you $2,000 up front, but you'll get a payback of lower monthly payments over the life of the loan. The money you pay for points is tax deductible. However, points paid to acquire a home are deductible in the year paid, while points paid to refinance a home are only deductible over the life of the mortgage.

The number of points charged will vary depending on the lender and the mortgage package. Points are paid at the closing.

Annual Percentage Rate (APR)

The *annual percentage rate (APR)* is the interest rate adjusted for loan fees and the term of the loan. This rate must be disclosed to borrowers under the Truth-In-Lending Act. Included in the rate are certain finance charges related to the mortgage, such as the loan origination fee, points and the loan interest rate. Because the APR includes these additional charges, buyers should use it to compare rates offered by different lenders—not simply the contract interest rate. The APR does not include costs such as credit reports, title fees, legal fees, survey fees, appraisal fees, and closing expenses.

Prequalifying versus Approval

Qualifying for a loan *before* you sign a contract on a home is commonly known as *prequalifying*. The process involves an analysis of income, debts, assets, credit rating and available cash—preferably by the lender who eventually will handle the mortgage. A buyer who has been prequalified can bid on any listed home up to a designated amount with the assurance that his or her mortgage loan will, for all practical purposes, be approved. And sellers may be more inclined to accept an offer from a buyer who has been prequalified for a loan.

Preapproved, on the other hand, means that the lender has actually made a commitment to lend a specified amount of money to the borrower on a particular property he or she wants to buy.

The Mortgage Commitment

If all systems are go, the lender is ready to issue the mortgage commitment. This commitment will be made in writing, stipulating the amount, interest rate and term of the mortgage. The borrower is then required to execute a note agreeing to repay the debt, and a mortgage or deed of trust placing a lien on the real estate to secure the note. The mortgage is then recorded to give notice of the lender's interest.

How *Your Agent Can Help*

Keeping up with the constantly shifting mortgage market is one of the real estate agent's most time-consuming jobs. A good real estate agent can give the buyer or seller up-to-date information on the different mortgage options available and which seem most appropriate for the buyer's needs. If the agent can't answer all the buyer's financial questions, he or she should be able to put the buyer in touch with someone who can. Experienced agents are also familiar with local lenders and can give competent advice about an institution's reputation, qualifying procedures and any unique benefits they offer homebuyers. The agent will then set up an application interview with the lender the buyer chooses. Some agents may even help buyers through the loan application process.

While the buyer is waiting for a mortgage commitment, both the seller's and buyer's agents expect to keep a close eye on the process, and to handle any problems that may come up. If the property "fails to appraise" and then the lender offers less than the amount the buyer needs, the agent may arrange for a re-appraisal, furnish comparable properties to back up the purchase price or even suggest that the buyer apply at a different financial institution. Frequently, the seller will be asked to renegotiate the contract.

Commonly Asked Questions

Q. How long does it take to approve a loan?

A. Normally it takes about 45 days for a loan application to be approved. The process can take more or less time, however, depending on the lender and the type of transaction involved.

Q. Do ARMs offer any protection against rising interest rates?

A. Yes. Most ARMs include provisions for the maximum amount your interest rate can rise, both annually and over the life of the loan. For example, if your initial rate is 5 percent, the loan may specify 2 percent annual and 6 percent lifetime caps. So even if interest rates rise dramatically, your rate can't increase more than 2 percent in any given year, and it can't rise above the lifetime maximum rate of 11 percent.

Q. Does the longer term mortgage have any tax advantage over the shorter term mortgage?

A. Yes. Interest on home mortgages is deductible. This means that the homeowner with the 30-year mortgage will get a much larger tax deduction than will the homeowner with a shorter term mortgage.

Q. How much do interest rates have to drop before refinancing is worth the expense?

A. Most mortgage experts agree that refinancing is a good investment if both of the following situations exist:

- You can get an interest rate of 2 percent lower than your existing rate. This is commonly referred to as the "2 percent rule."
- You plan to stay in your home for at least 18 months. In general, the longer you plan to stay in your home, the more sense it makes to refinance.

Q. Can I assume a VA loan if I'm not a veteran?

A. Yes. Anyone, even those who are not veterans, can assume a VA loan. Some older VA loans do not require the lender's approval. Newer VA loans can be assumed only with the lender's approval.

CHAPTER 11

Closing the Deal

The term *closing* refers to the final step in the process of buying or selling a house. It is the time when title to the property is transferred from the seller to the buyer.

Closings may be conducted by title companies, escrow agents, lending institutions, attorneys and, in some areas, by real estate brokers. They may take place at a title company, a bank, an attorney's office or some other location.

Those attending a closing may include:

- The buyer
- The seller
- The real estate agent or broker (from the selling and listing offices)
- Attorneys for the seller and buyer
- Representatives and attorneys for lending institutions involved with the buyer's new mortgage loan, the

buyer's assumption of the seller's existing loan or the
seller's payoff of an existing loan
• The representative of the title insurance company

The Closing Statement

Every real estate transaction that involves the transfer of
property requires the preparation of a written form called a
closing statement or *settlement statement.* The closing
statement is a way of calculating the amount owed by the
buyer as well as the net amount that the seller will receive.
A sample closing statement form is shown in Figure 11.1.

The completion of a closing statement involves an
accounting of the buyer's and seller's debits and credits. A
debit is a charge—an amount that the person owes and must
pay at the closing. A *credit* is an amount entered in a
person's favor—either an amount that has already been paid,
that is being reimbursed or that the buyer promises to pay
in the form of a loan.

The overall equations for closing statements are:

Buyer's charges (debits) – Buyer's credits = Cash buyer
owes at closing

Seller's credits – Seller's charges (debits) = Cash seller will
receive at closing

In other words: A *debit* takes money from; a *credit* gives
money to.

Finding the Bottom Line for the Buyer and Seller

Refer to the closing statement worksheet in Figure 11.2 as
you read. To determine the amount the buyer needs at the
closing, add all of the buyer's debits together; these include
any expenses and prorated amounts for items prepaid by the
seller. Add this number to the purchase price. Then add

FIGURE 11.1 Closing Statement

SELLER'S CREDITS				
Sale Price				$ 89,500.00
ADJUSTMENT OF TAXES				
School Tax to	Amt. $ 1176.35	Adj. 10 mos. 18 days		1,039.16
City/School Tax to	Amt. $ _____	Adj.. ___ mos. ___ days		_____
County Tax 19____	Amt. $ 309.06	Adj. 4 mos. 18 days		118.52
Village Tax to	Amt. $ _____	Adj. ___ mos. ___ days		_____
City Tax Embellishments	Amt. $ _____	Adj. ___ mos. ___ days		_____

Total Seller's Credits $ 90,657.68

PURCHASER'S CREDITS

	$ 500.00
Deposit with Nothnagle	$ 40,000.00
(Assumed) (New) Mortgage with seller	$ _____
12% interest, 15 years, payments	$ _____
$480.07, beginning	$ _____
	$ _____
	$ _____
	$ _____ $

Total Purchaser's Credits $ 40,500.00

Cash (Rec's) (Paid) at Closing   50,157.68

EXPENSES OF PURCHASER		EXPENSES OF SELLER	
Mortgage Tax	$ _____	Title Search Fee	$ 220.00
Recording Mortgage	$ _____	Transfer Tax on Deed	$ 358.00
Recording Deed	$ _____	Filing Gains Tax Affidavit	$ 1.00
ESCROWS: $ _____		Discharge Recording Fee	$ _____
___ mos. insurance	$ _____	Mortgage Tax	$ 100.00
___ mos. school tax	$ _____	Surveyor's Fees	$ _____
___ mos. county tax	$ _____	Points	$ _____
___ mos. village tax	$ _____	Mortgage Payoff	$ _____
PMI FHA Insurance	$ _____	Real Estate Commission	$ 487.00
Total	$ _____	Water Escrow	$ _____
Bank Attorney Fee	$ _____	19 school tax	$ 1,182.14
Points	$ _____	Federal Express	$ 14.00
Title Insurance	$ _____	....	$ _____
Interest	$ _____	....	$ _____
....	$ _____	Legal Fee	$ 550.00
....	$ _____	Total	$ 7,295.14
....	$ _____	Cash Received:	$ 50,157.68
Legal Fee	$ _____	Less Seller's Expenses:	$ 7,295.14
Total	$ _____	Net Proceeds:	$ 42,862.54
Cash paid to Seller:	$ _____		
Plus Purchaser's Expenses:	$ _____		
Total Disbursed:	$ _____		

FIGURE 11.2 Closing StatementWorksheet

	Buyer's Statement		Seller's Statement	
	Debit	Credit	Debit	Credit
Purchase price	$135,000			$135,000
Earnest money		$ 6,000		
Assumed loan balance		87,500	$ 87,500	
Interest on assumed loan		306	306	
Real estate taxes through closing date		1,427	1,427	
Tax reserve	1,986			1,986
Insurance premium proration	1,052			1,052
Buyer's expenses:				
Assumption fee	875			
Recording fee	25			
Seller's expenses				
Title search			1,350	
Broker's commission			9,450	
Transfer tax			47	
Subtotal	138,938	95,233	100,080	138,038
Due from buyer		43,705		
Due to seller			37,958	
Totals	**$138,938**	**$138,938**	**$138,038**	**$138,038**

together all of the buyer's credits; these include the earnest money deposit (already paid), the balance of the loan the buyer is obtaining or assuming and the seller's share of any prorated items that the buyer will pay in the future. Subtract the total credits from the total amount the buyer owes (debits). You have now determined the actual amount of cash the buyer must bring to the closing. Usually, the buyer will bring a certified check for the balance of the cash needed to complete the purchase.

A similar procedure is followed to determine how much money the seller will actually receive. The seller's debits and credits are each totaled. The credits include the purchase price plus the buyer's share of any prorated items that the seller has prepaid. The seller's debits include expenses, the seller's share of prorated items to be paid later by the buyer and the balance of any mortgage loan or other lien that the seller is paying off. Finally, the total of the seller's charges or debits is subtracted from the total credits to arrive at the amount the seller will receive.

Types of Entries

Following are items that must be accounted for in a closing statement, grouped by type of entry and how each is typically debited or credited. Local customs and practices may differ.

Note: If you are not familiar with some of these terms, check the glossary at the back of the book.

Sales price. This is debited to the buyer and credited to the seller.

Earnest money. This is credited only to the buyer. The buyer receives a credit because he or she has already paid that amount toward the sales price.

Proceeds of a new mortgage obtained by the buyer. This is credited to the buyer *without* a corresponding debit to the seller, because the buyer receives this money from the lender. The seller's existing mortgage must then be paid off by a debit to the seller.

Balance of assumed loan and accrued interest. This is debited to the seller and credited to the buyer.

Purchase-money loan. This is credited to the buyer, who assumes an obligation for future payments; it also is debited to the seller, who accepts the note in lieu of cash.

Prorations. This is debited to one party and credited to the other. Items debited to the buyer and credited to the seller include the following:

- Prepaid real estate taxes
- Insurance and tax reserve escrow account balance
- Coal or fuel oil on hand
- Prepaid utilities
- Personal property purchased by the buyer

Items debited to the seller and credited to the buyer include the following:

- Principal of loan assumed by the buyer
- Accrued interest on existing assumed loan not yet payable
- Accrued portion of real estate tax not yet due

Other items may be included, depending on the customs of your area.

Expenses charged to seller or buyer. This is to be paid out of the closing proceeds and are debited only to the party making the payment.

Debits to the seller include the following:

- Broker's commission
- Legal fee for drawing the deed
- Title expenses required by the sales contract
- Loan discount points
- Repairs (as required by the sales contract)
- Loan payoff fees
- Filing fee for release of lien
- Loan discount fees (if required by the lender and as negotiated in the sales contract)

Debits to the buyer include the following:

- Assumption or transfer fee (when the buyer assumes an existing loan)
- Survey (if required by the lender)
- Recording fees for deed and mortgage
- Loan origination fee
- Certified copies of deed restrictions
- Credit report
- Prepaid taxes, insurance and interest
- Mortgage insurance premium (when required by the lender)
- Flood insurance premium/homeowners insurance premium
- Appraisal fee
- Termite, structural, mechanical and environmental inspections (Termite inspection is a charge to the seller in transactions with a VA-guaranteed loan.)

Debits to the party responsible or shared by seller and buyer include the following:

- Transfer tax
- Cost of title insurance or title examination
- Legal fees
- Escrow fee
- Inspection fees

Other items may be included, depending on the customs of your area and the provisions of the sales contract.

Uniform Settlement Statement

Normally, each company performing a closing will use its own printed form. An exception to this practice occurs when the purchase is financed with a federally related mortgage loan. In such cases, the closing is regulated by the

Real Estate Settlement Procedures Act (RESPA). The large majority of mortgage loans falls under these requirements. All transactions covered by RESPA must use the Uniform Settlement Statement (HUD Form 1) as the closing document. A copy of this form is shown in Figure 11.3. Page 2 of the HUD form must be completed first because detailed items are summarized on page 1. Also, the term *debit* is not used; the HUD form merely says "paid from borrower's/ seller's funds." The seller should always request a copy of the statement 24 hours (or more) prior to close.

Breakdown of the HUD Form

Sections A through I of the HUD settlement statement contain information about the loan and parties to the settlement.

Sections J and K contain a summary of all funds transferred between the borrower, seller, lender and providers of settlement services. The bottom line in the left-hand column shows the net cash to be paid by the buyer; the bottom line in the right-hand column shows the cash due the seller.

Section L is a list of settlement charges that may be required from the buyer and seller. Blank lines are provided at the end of the list for any additional settlement charges.

The costs entered on the lines of Section L are added up; the totals are then carried forward to the bottom lines of the left and right columns of Sections J and K, in order to arrive at the net cash figures.

Figure 11.4 is a checklist of things to do during the final weerk in your home.

FIGURE 11.3 RESPA Uniform Settlement Statement

RESPA UNIFORM SETTLEMENT STATEMENT

A. Settlement Statement

U.S. Department of Housing
and Urban Development

OMB Approval No. 2502-0265

B. Type of Loan

1. ☐ FHA 2. ☐ FmHA 3. ☐ Conv. Unins. 4. ☐ VA 5. ☐ Conv. Ins.

6. File Number	7. Loan Number	8. Mortgage Insurance Case Number

C. Note: This form is furnished to give you a statement of actual settlement costs. Amounts paid to and by the settlement agent are shown. Items marked "(p.o.c.)" were paid outside the closing; they are shown here for informational purposes and are not included in the totals.

D. Name and Address of Borrower	E. Name and Address of Seller	F. Name and Address of Lender

G. Property Location	H. Settlement Agent	
	Place of Settlement	I. Settlement Date

J. Summary of Borrower's Transaction		K. Summary of Seller's Transaction	
100. Gross Amount Due From Borrower		**400. Gross Amount Due To Seller**	
101. Contract sales price		401. Contract sales price	
102. Personal property		402. Personal property	
103. Settlement charges to borrower (line 1400)		403.	
104.		404.	
105.		405.	
Adjustments for items paid by seller in advance		**Adjustments for items paid by seller in advance**	
106. City/town taxes to		406. City/town taxes to	
107. County taxes to		407. County taxes to	
108. Assessments to		408. Assessments to	
109.		409.	
110.		410.	
111.		411.	
112.		412.	
120. Gross Amount Due From Borrower		**420. Gross Amount Due To Seller**	
200. Amounts Paid By Or In Behalf Of Borrower		**500. Reductions In Amount Due To Seller**	
201. Deposit or earnest money		501. Excess deposit (see instructions)	
202. Principal amount of new loan(s)		502. Settlement charges to seller (line 1400)	
203. Existing loan(s) taken subject to		503. Existing loan(s) taken subject to	
204.		504. Payoff of first mortgage loan	
205.		505. Payoff of second mortgage loan	
206.		506.	
207.		507.	
208.		508.	
209.		509.	
Adjustments for items unpaid by seller		**Adjustments for items unpaid by seller**	
210. City/town taxes to		510. City/town taxes to	
211. County taxes to		511. County taxes to	
212. Assessments to		512. Assessments to	
213.		513.	
214.		514.	
215.		515.	
216.		516.	
217.		517.	
218.		518.	
219.		519.	
220. Total Paid By/For Borrower		**520. Total Reduction Amount Due Seller**	
300. Cash At Settlement From/To Borrower		**600. Cash At Settlement To/From Seller**	
301. Gross Amount due from borrower (line 120)		601. Gross amount due to seller (line 420)	
302. Less amounts paid by/for borrower (line 220)	( )	602. Less reductions in amt. due seller (line 520)	( )
303. Cash ☐ From ☐ To Borrower		**603. Cash** ☐ To ☐ From Seller	

FIGURE 11.3 RESPA Uniform Settlement Statement (Continued)

L. Settlement Charges			Paid From Borrowers Funds at Settlement	Paid From Seller's Funds at Settlement
700. Total Sales/Broker's Commission based on price $	@	% =		
Division of Commission (line 700) as follows:				
701. $	to			
702. $	to			
703. Commission paid at Settlement				
704.				
800. Items Payable In Connection With Loan				
801. Loan Origination Fee	%			
802. Loan Discount	%			
803. Appraisal Fee	to			
804. Credit Report	to			
805. Lender's Inspection Fee				
806. Mortgage Insurance Application Fee to				
807. Assumption Fee				
808.				
809.				
810.				
811.				
900. Items Required By Lender To Be Paid In Advance				
901. Interest from to @$	/day			
902. Mortgage Insurance Premium for	months to			
903. Hazard Insurance Premium for	years to			
904.	years to			
905.				
1000. Reserves Deposited With Lender				
1001. Hazard insurance	months@$	per month		
1002. Mortgage insurance	months@$	per month		
1003. City property taxes	months@$	per month		
1004. County property taxes	months@$	per month		
1005. Annual assessments	months@$	per month		
1006.	months@$	per month		
1007.	months@$	per month		
1008.	months@$	per month		
1100. Title Charges				
1101. Settlement or closing fee	to			
1102. Abstract or title search	to			
1103. Title examination	to			
1104. Title insurance binder	to			
1105. Document preparation	to			
1106. Notary fees	to			
1107. Attorney's fees	to			
(includes above items numbers:	)			
1108. Title insurance	to			
(includes above items numbers:	)			
1109. Lender's coverage	$			
1110. Owner's coverage	$			
1111.				
1112.				
1113.				
1200. Government Recording and Transfer Charges				
1201. Recording fees: Deed $	; Mortgage $	; Releases $		
1202. City/county tax/stamps: Deed $	; Mortgage $			
1203. State tax/stamps: Deed $	; Mortgage $			
1204.				
1205.				
1300. Additional Settlement Charges				
1301. Survey to				
1302. Pest inspection to				
1303.				
1304.				
1305.				
1400. Total Settlement Charges (enter on lines 103, Section J and 502, Section K)				

Public Reporting Burden for this collection of information is estimated to average 0.25 hours per response, including the time for reviewing instructions, searching existing data sources, gathering and maintaining the data needed, and completing and reviewing the collection of information. Send comments regarding this burden estimate or any other aspect of this collection of information, including suggestions for reducing this burden, to the Reports Management Officer, Office of Information Policies and Systems, U.S. Department of Housing and Urban Development, Washington, D.C. 20410-3600, and to the Office of Management and Budget, Paperwork Reduction Project (2502-0265), Washington, D.C. 20503

FIGURE 11.4 Checklist: Things to Do Before Closing

❏ Confirm the closing date, time and place.

❏ Review the contract and make sure any items on which the closing is contingent have been taken care of.

❏ Determine whether all the required repairs have been made.

❏ Arrange with utility companies to shut off all water, gas and electricity in your name and to issue final bills to your new address.

❏ At the same time, the buyer should notify the utility companies of the purchase, so that service will be continued in the buyer's name.

❏ Arrange to have the post office forward your mail to your new address.

❏ Cancel newspaper subscriptions and cable TV service.

❏ Have your phone disconnected.

❏ Check with your agent to verify that all necessary paperwork will be ready for the closing.

❏ Have your agent get you a copy of your estimated closing costs. Go over the statement with your agent to see that all figures are correct.

❏ Make sure you have all the documents you are expected to bring to the closing—such as paid real estate tax receipts, survey and a copy of your mortgage and any other liens on the property.

❏ After the closing, call your insurance agent and cancel your homeowners policy.

How Your Agent Can Help

An agent can be a valuable source of advice at the closing—especially if any last-minute problems arise.

A good agent also will help you prepare for the closing by giving you a step-by-step preview of the entire process and what will be expected of you. He or she will make sure all pertinent documents and other items are available before the specified closing date. For example, the title insurance or title certificate, surveys, property insurance policy and other items must be ordered and reviewed; and closing statements and other documents must be prepared.

Commonly Asked Questions

Q. Will the closing be on the exact date stated in the contract?

A. In most cases, the day specified in the contract is simply a target date. If that date is not met, the contract is still in force, as long as both parties have agreed to a new date. When the buyer's lender has committed the mortgage loan funds, the person in charge of the closing can arrange a date that is suitable to all parties.

Q. Is it acceptable to let the buyers move in before closing?

A. Don't let it happen if you can help it. You might find yourself with a mess on your hands if for some reason the closing doesn't go through as planned.

For example, if the buyer moves in before closing, you give him or her the opportunity to find things wrong with the house. At best, you could wind up paying lots of money for repairs. At worst, the buyer could cancel the sale and you'd be stuck with the time and expense involved in finding a new buyer.

Letting the buyer move in before he or she takes legal possession of the home can lead to other problems. For example, if the buyer or a visitor is injured on the property while you still own it, you could be held liable. Or, what would happen if the buyer's loan application is rejected and he or she refuses to move out?

When you look at all the negative things that could happen, letting the buyer move into your house before the sale is completed is just too risky.

Q. How long does a closing typically take?

A. Most closings are over in an hour. Real estate agents try to explain everything to the buyers and sellers beforehand so there are no surprises at the closing.

```
┌─────────────────────────┐
│  ┌───────────────────┐  │
│  │   CHAPTER 12      │  │
│  └───────────────────┘  │
└─────────────────────────┘
```

Tax Consequences after the Sale

If you sell a home and make a profit, your gain is potentially taxable; that is, the Internal Revenue Service (IRS) may be entitled to part of the money you make.

In this chapter, we're going to take a brief look at some of the tax issues involved in a home sale. However, for specific tax advice and up-to-date information, be sure to consult with a competent tax adviser when you sell your home. Do not rely on this chapter to help you plan or prepare your taxes.

Selling Your Home at a Loss

While the IRS potentially taxes profits from the sale of a home, it generally does not allow you to deduct losses. It doesn't seem fair, but that's the way it is.

Selling Your Home at a Profit

The IRS offers two major tax shelters for profit on the sale of your primary home: the rollover and the one-time exclusion.

Rollover

Rolling over your profit means postponing tax on all or part of your gain when one home is sold and replaced within two years by another. With this option, if you buy a replacement house of equal or greater value than the one you sold, you can postpone the payment of taxes on all of the profit. If you are selling a home and buying another that is less expensive, you may still defer part of the tax on the profit. Only that portion of the profit not offset by the cost of the replacement home will be taxed.

You do not eliminate the tax on your profit by rolling it over, however; you simply defer it until your next home is sold. You can continue to pile up untaxed profit as long as you continue to trade up, that is, when you replace each house you sell with one that is more expensive.

One-Time Exclusion

With this tax-shelter option, you can continue to defer any tax liability until you trade down. At this time, you may owe some taxes, or you may be able to take the one-time exclusion on profit up to $125,000 with no federal tax due ever. The $125,000 limit also can include untaxed profits from previous homes. You can claim this exclusion only once, and only if you are 55 years of age or older on the date of sale. If you're married, only one spouse has to be 55. In addition, you must have owned and occupied the house as a principal residence for at least three of the five years before the sale.

For more information on the $125,000 exclusion and other tax benefits and requirements, call the IRS and ask them to send you a free copy of Publication 523, "Tax Information on Selling Your Home."

☞ **Money-$aving Tip #46** *If you qualify, the $125,000 exclusion can include untaxed profit on previous homes for which you rolled over your gain.*

Figuring Your Gain When You Sell Your House

Because the profit on the sale of your house involves the sale of an asset, the IRS classifies it as a *capital gain*. If you are not using one of the special tax breaks allowed by the IRS, your profit will be taxed at whatever capital gains rates apply at the time you sell.

Computing the amount of the gain when you sell your house is a three-step process:

Step 1: Find the Adjusted Cost Basis on the Home You Are Selling

According to the IRS, a property's *cost basis* determines the amount of gain to be taxed. Cost basis is the purchase price of the home plus the costs of buying it, such as closing costs and certain loan costs.

The cost basis can be increased by any improvements you make to the property. Improvements are replacements or additions that increase the property's value. Examples include adding a room, roof, siding, swimming pool, patio, deck, garage, fireplace, insulation and central air-conditioning.

The IRS allows you to add the cost of improvements to the cost basis for your property to arrive at what is known as the *adjusted cost basis*. You'll see later that the higher the cost basis, the smaller your taxable gain will be when you sell.

The IRS takes a different view, however, when it comes to repairs and maintenance. Repairs and maintenance—and you can include redecorating—simply *preserve* the condition of the property and cannot be used to increase the cost basis. That is, they have no effect on your tax liability. Repairs and maintenance include such things as painting, wallpapering, patching the roof, fixing leaks, repairing gutters and resealing the driveway.

It's important, therefore, for you to know the difference between improvements and normal repairs and maintenance. Sometimes the distinction is clear. Replacing a few bad shingles on a roof is a repair; reshingling the entire roof is an improvement. In some cases, however, only a fine line separates an improvement from a repair or maintenance. Repapering a bedroom, for example, is simply redecoration. On the other hand, wallpapering a new room addition is an improvement. If you are in doubt as to whether a specific expenditure you have made is an improvement or a normal repair, contact the IRS.

In addition to the money you've spent for permanent improvements, you can add to your cost basis special tax assessments paid over the years for items like sidewalks, sewers or street lights.

Following is an example of how the adjusted cost basis can be calculated:

Purchase price	$100,000
Costs of buying	+ 8,000
Cost basis	$108,000
Cost of improvements	+ 20,000
Cost of Assessments	+ -0-
Adjusted cost basis	$128,000

Caution: To get any tax benefit from the IRS, it is important to keep accurate records of any improvements you make or assessments you have received and how much they cost. You should also keep records of the costs you paid at closing on both the house you are selling and the house you are buying.

☞ **Money-$aving Tip #47** *Good records will help you save tax dollars.*

☞ **Money-$aving Tip #48** *The higher the cost basis for your house, the smaller your taxable gain will be when you sell. The cost basis can be increased by the following:*
- *Any permanent improvements made to the property*
- *Any special tax assessments paid over the years (not property tax assessments)*
- *The costs of buying the house, such as closing costs and certain loan costs*

Step 2: Find the Adjusted Sales Price

Just as you adjusted the cost basis for your house, you will need to adjust the sales price, subtracting from it certain costs of selling to arrive at the adjusted sales price. The IRS calls the adjusted sales price the amount *realized.*

The largest of the selling costs will probably be the real estate commission—if you sell through an agent. You also can deduct legal fees, costs of proving title and other costs of actually making the sale.

Following is an example of how the adjusted sales price can be calculated:

Sales price	$175,000
Costs of selling	– 16,000
Adjusted sales price	$159,000

☞ **Money-$aving Tip #49** *Be sure to deduct costs of selling to arrive at your adjusted sales price. This will reduce the taxable gain on the sale.*

Step 3: Figure the Gain on the Sale

Your gain or profit on the sale is your adjusted sales price minus your adjusted cost basis:

Adjusted sales price	$159,000
Adjusted cost basis	-128,000
Taxable gain on sale	$ 31,000

Following is an example of how to calculate the cost basis on your replacement home:

Purchase price of replacement home	$225,000
Costs of buying	- 11,000
Amount of deferred tax	- 31,000
Cost basis of replacement home	$183,000

Notice that the amount of deferred tax is subtracted from the purchase price in determining the cost basis of the new house. Of course, this reduction will increase the amount of taxable gain at some later date if the funds from the sale of this new house are not reinvested in yet another principal residence.

Purchasing a Less Expensive Replacement Home

If the replacement house does not have a cost basis that is at least equal to the adjusted sales price of the house that has been sold at a gain, the tax is only partially deferred.

Adjusted sales price (from step 2, page 125)	$159,000
Cost basis of replacement house	-150,000
Taxable gain	9,000
Total taxable gain (from step 3, above)	$ 31,000
Taxable gain	- 9,000
Amount of taxable gain deferred	$ 22,000
Cost basis of replacement house	$150,000
Amount of deferred tax	- 22,000
Cost basis of replacement house	$128,000

Reporting the Sale of Your Home

The sale of your home will be reported to the IRS on Form 1099 by the party in charge of the closing—even if no tax is due. You will probably be asked to give your Social Security number and your new address at closing so that a copy of the 1099 can be sent to you.

In the year that you sell, you are required to report the sale on Form 2119 and attach it to your income tax return. This provides the IRS with a matching form from you to go with the 1099 received from the closing.

Form 2119 guides you through the steps involved in calculating taxable and postponed profit. If you intend to buy a replacement residence within the two-year period but have not yet done so when you file your tax return, you can choose one of two options:

1. You can pay tax on your profit now and, if and when you buy a house within the time limit, file an amended return for a refund of the tax paid plus interest.
2. You can state your intention to buy a replacement home, not pay tax, and then amend your return, detailing the replacement you do buy. If in the end you do not purchase a replacement, you would owe the tax that would have been due, plus interest.

☞ **Money-$aving Tip #50** *Consulting your tax adviser before the sale can be very profitable time well spent.*

How Your Agent Can Help

The tax implications of a home sale can be confusing. Although the information in this chapter should give you a general idea of how the system works, it shouldn't be relied on for specific tax guidance. For advice and information that is appropriate for your particular situation, you may need to consult with a tax adviser. If you don't have a tax adviser, your agent can give you the names of several competent ones in the area.

Commonly Asked Questions

Q. Do I have to report the sale of my home on my income tax return even if no tax is due on the profit?

A. Yes. If you don't, your return will not match the 1099 the IRS receives.

Q. Suppose I'm over 55 and I sell my home for a $75,000 profit. Can I write off the $75,000 now and at some later time write off the remaining $50,000?

A. No. The over-55 rule can be used only once. If you write off $75,000, that's it.

Q. Do I get a tax break for the cost of repairs made to my house prior to selling it?

A. Repairs made 90 days prior to a sale and paid for within 30 days of closing can be deducted from the adjusted sales price only in figuring the part of the gain that you postpone. You cannot deduct repairs in figuring the actual gain on the house you sold.

Q. *Can I get a deduction if I sell my home at a loss?*

A. You cannot deduct a loss on the sale of a personal residence on your income tax return.

Q. *How is my profit taxed if I can't use the special tax breaks allowed by the IRS?*

A. Your profit will be taxed at whatever capital gains rates apply at the time you sell.

CHAPTER 13

Using Today's Technology to Help

Whether they are laptop or desktop models, computers have become an integral tool for real estate brokers and agents. Computers can save agents time by calculating complex financing deals or sifting through vast databases to find a handful of homes for a potential buyer.

Many agents use personal computers connected to a computer at their local Board of REALTORS®. The computer maintains all active property listings and sales information on properties, including homes, condominiums, commercial properties and vacant land. It also updates this data for each office in the network and gives agents a chance to exchange messages.

In addition to reducing the time it takes to do complex figuring, computers also reduce the chance for human error.

Computer Terminology

To understand the impact of computers on the real estate industry, you should be familiar with certain computer terms:

- *Cyberspace.* The imaginary place where people communicate and view text and pictures using their personal computers.
- *Internet.* A worldwide community of people using computers to interact. It is a way to get information on a variety of topics.
- *Modem.* A device that translates digital information into signals that can be transmitted between computers over telephone lines.
- *World Wide Web.* An Internet tool that allows users to view "home pages" that can include text, photographs and sound.
- *Home page.* A site on the World Wide Web that serves to introduce an organization or individual to other users. By clicking on underlined "hypertext" words on the home page, users can see "links," or related pages, or access e-mail and other services.
- *Online.* Using computers to access information from other computers via telephone lines and modems.

Real Estate Online

The Internet's World Wide Web is the newest of many tools real estate companies use to market properties.

The open house remains an effective way by which real estate brokers and agents can publicize themselves and the properties they represent. It provides the broker or agent with the opportunity to show the property and to discuss its features. Most important, however, the broker or agent can gather input from prospective buyers. What's new as we approach the 21st century is that many brokers and agents are holding an open house without setting foot on the property. Instead, many are putting their listings—and information about their companies—on the World Wide Web, where they're holding "virtual" open houses. There, prospective buyers across the world can view neighborhoods and homes via personal computers and modems. They can see street maps, property tax figures and other public information and census data for any particular area that interests them.

Using today's technology, brokers and agents can present listing information and photographs of houses right in the prospective buyer's living room on a laptop computer. With a few keystrokes, it's possible to view photos and text describing a $5 million estate in England or a charming little house in North Carolina for under $100,000.

The new technology not only helps the buyer, but it helps the seller too. When listing a house, the broker and seller gain an edge in the marketplace if they can view online photographs and listing information of nearby houses on the market. Such information can help them set a competitive list price.

And the broker can include, with the photos and listing information, a map of the property's location, with the capability of transmitting the listing to hundreds of other REALTORS® in the area, as well as nationally.

How Your Agent Can Help

More and more real estate offices can guide buyers through the Internet's World Wide Web to assist with their house-hunting. As great as it is to sit at home or at a broker's office and look at houses on a computer screen, it's highly unlikely you or anyone else is going to buy a home without leaving cyberspace and visiting real space.

While brokers and agents have embraced pagers, cellular phones and computers, buying and selling real estate is still a person-to-person interaction. The key to buying or selling a house—as always—is a broker or agent who knows the market and will work seven days a week to help you. And, a computer will never replace personal service.

Commonly Asked Questions

Q. Do any companies provide online computer listings of homes that are for sale?

A. All three of the country's major online services—Prodigy, America Online and CompuServe—offer computerized databases of properties that are for sale.

It's important to remember, however, that these databases feature only a small fraction of all the homes that are for sale in a given area. Most sellers and agents still market their properties the conventional way, using yard signs and taking out advertisements in local newspapers.

Sample Disclosure Statement

136   Appendix A

REAL ESTATE TRANSFER DISCLOSURE STATEMENT
(CALIFORNIA CIVIL CODE 1102, ET SEQ.)
CALIFORNIA ASSOCIATION OF REALTORS® (CAR) STANDARD FORM

THIS DISCLOSURE STATEMENT CONCERNS THE REAL PROPERTY SITUATED IN THE CITY OF_____
_____, COUNTY OF_____, STATE OF CALIFORNIA,
DESCRIBED AS_____.
THIS STATEMENT IS A DISCLOSURE OF THE CONDITION OF THE ABOVE DESCRIBED PROPERTY IN COMPLIANCE
WITH SECTION 1102 OF THE CIVIL CODE AS OF _____, 19____. IT IS NOT A WARRANTY
OF ANY KIND BY THE SELLER(S) OR ANY AGENT(S) REPRESENTING ANY PRINCIPAL(S) IN THIS TRANSACTION,
AND IS NOT A SUBSTITUTE FOR ANY INSPECTIONS OR WARRANTIES THE PRINCIPAL(S) MAY WISH TO OBTAIN.

I
COORDINATION WITH OTHER DISCLOSURE FORMS

This Real Estate Transfer Disclosure Statement is made pursuant to Section 1102 of the Civil Code. Other statutes require disclosures, depending upon the details of the particular real estate transaction (for example: special study zone and purchase-money liens on residential property).

Substituted Disclosures: The following disclosures have or will be in connection with this real estate transfer, and are intended o satisfy the disclosure obligations on this form, where the subject matter is the same: _____

_____
_____

(LIST ALL SUBSTITUTED DISCLOSURE FORMS TO BE USED IN CONNECTION WITH THIS TRANSACTION)

II
SELLER'S INFORMATION

The Seller discloses the following information with the knowledge that even though this is not a warranty, prospective Buyers may rely on this information in deciding whether and on what terms to purchase the subject property. Seller hereby authorizes any agent(s) representing any principal(s) in this transaction to provide a copy of this statement to any person or entity in connection with any actual or anticipated sale of the property.

THE FOLLOWING ARE REPRESENTATIONS MADE BY THE SELLER(S) AND ARE NOT THE REPRESENTATIONS OF THE AGENT(S), IF ANY. THIS INFORMATION IS A DISCLOSURE AND IS NOT INTENDED TO BE PART OF ANY CONTRACT BETWEEN THE BUYER AND SELLER.

Seller ☐ is ☐ is not occupying the property.

A. The subject property has the items checked below (read across):

☐ Range	☐ Oven	☐ Microwave
☐ Dishwasher	☐ Trash Compactor	☐ Garbage Disposal
☐ Washer/Dryer Hookups	☐ Window Screens	☐ Rain Gutters
☐ Burglar Alarms	☐ Smoke Detector(s)	☐ Fire Alarm
☐ T.V. Antenna	☐ Satellite Dish	☐ Intercom
☐ Central Heating	☐ Central Air Conditioning	☐ Evaporator Cooler(s)
☐ Wall/Window Air Conditioning	☐ Sprinklers	☐ Public Sewer System
☐ Septic Tank	☐ Sump Pump	☐ Water Softener
☐ Patio/Decking	☐ Built-in Barbeque	☐ Gazebo
☐ Sauna	☐ Pool	☐ Spa ☐ Hot Tub
☐ Security Gate(s)	☐ Automatic Garage Door Opener(s)*	☐ Number of Remote Controls____
Garage: ☐ Attached	☐ Not Attached	☐ Carport
Pool/Spa Heater: ☐ Gas	☐ Solar	☐ Electric
Water Heater: ☐ Gas	☐ Solar	☐ Electric
Water Supply: ☐ City	☐ Well	☐ Private Utility ☐ Other____
Gas Supply: ☐ Utility	☐ Bottled	

Exhaust Fan(s) in_____220 Volt Wiring in_____
Fireplace(s) in_____ ☐ Gas Starter
☐ Roof(s): Type:_____Age:_____(approx.)
☐ Other:_____
Are there, to the best of your (Seller's) knowledge, any of the above that are not in operating condition? ☐ Yes ☐ No If yes, then describe. (Attach additional sheets if necessary.):_____
_____
_____

B. Are you (Seller) aware of any significant defects/malfunctions in any of the following? ☐ Yes ☐ No If yes, check appropriate space(s) below.
☐ Interior Walls ☐ Ceilings ☐ Floors ☐ Exterior Walls ☐ Insulation ☐ Roof(s) ☐ Windows ☐ Doors ☐ Foundation ☐ Slab(s)
☐ Driveways ☐ Sidewalks ☐ Walls/Fences ☐ Electrical Systems ☐ Plumbing/Sewers/Septics ☐ Other Structural Components
(Describe:_____
_____
_____)

If any of the above is checked, explain. (Attach additional sheets if necessary):_____
_____
_____

*This garage door opener may not be in compliance with the safety standards relating to automatic reversing devices as set forth in Chapter 12.5 (commencing with Section 19890) of Part 3 of Division 13 of the Health and Safety Code.
Buyer and Seller acknowledge receipt of copy of this page, which constitutes Page 1 of 2 Pages.
Buyer's Initials (_____) (_____) Seller's Initials (_____) (_____)

Copyright © 1990, CALIFORNIA ASSOCIATION OF REALTORS®
525 South Virgil Avenue, Los Angeles, California 90020
IN COMPLIANCE WITH CIVIL CODE SECTION 1102.6 / EFFECTIVE JULY 1, 1991.

BROKER'S COPY

OFFICE USE ONLY
Reviewed by Broker or Designee _____
Date _____

EQUAL HOUSING OPPORTUNITY

M-PM-5/94

REAL ESTATE TRANSFER DISCLOSURE STATEMENT (TDS-14 PAGE 1 OF 2)

☐

Subject Property Address: _____ _____ , 19 _____

C. Are you (Seller) aware of any of the following:

1. Substances, materials, or products which may be an environmental hazard such as, but not limited to, asbestos, formaldehyde, radon gas, lead-based paint, fuel or chemical storage tanks, and contaminated soil or water on the subject property. . . . . ☐ Yes ☐ No
2. Features of the property shared in common with adjoining landowners, such as walls, fences, and driveways, whose use or responsibility for maintenance may have an effect on the subject property. ☐ Yes ☐ No
3. Any encroachments, easements or similar matters that may affect your interest in the subject property. . . . . ☐ Yes ☐ No
4. Room additions, structural modifications, or other alterations or repairs made without necessary permits. . . . . . . ☐ Yes ☐ No
5. Room additions, structural modifications, or other alterations or repairs not in compliance with building codes. . . . ☐ Yes ☐ No
6. Landfill (compacted or otherwise) on the property or any portion thereof. . . . . ☐ Yes ☐ No
7. Any settling from any cause, or slippage, sliding, or other soil problems. . . . . ☐ Yes ☐ No
8. Flooding, drainage or grading problems. . . . . ☐ Yes ☐ No
9. Major damage to the property or any of the structures from fire, earthquake, floods, or landslides. . . . . ☐ Yes ☐ No
10. Any zoning violations, nonconforming uses, violations of "setback" requirements. . . . . ☐ Yes ☐ No
11. Neighborhood noise problems or other nuisances. . . . . ☐ Yes ☐ No
12. CC&R's or other deed restrictions or obligations. . . . . ☐ Yes ☐ No
13. Homeowners' Association which has any authority over the subject property. . . . . ☐ Yes ☐ No
14. Any "common area" (facilities such as pools, tennis courts, walkways, or other areas co-owned in undivided interest with others). . . . . ☐ Yes ☐ No
15. Any notices of abatement or citations against the property. . . . . ☐ Yes ☐ No
16. Any lawsuits against the seller threatening to or affecting this real property. . . . . ☐ Yes ☐ No

If the answer to any of these is yes, explain. (Attach additional sheets if necessary.):_____
_____
_____

Seller certifies that the information herein is true and correct to the best of the Seller's knowledge as of the date signed by the Seller.

Seller_____ Date_____

Seller_____ Date_____

III
AGENT'S INSPECTION DISCLOSURE
(To be completed only if the seller is represented by an agent in this transaction.)
THE UNDERSIGNED, BASED ON THE ABOVE INQUIRY OF THE SELLER(S) AS TO THE CONDITION OF THE PROPERTY AND BASED ON A REASONABLY COMPETENT AND DILIGENT VISUAL INSPECTION OF THE ACCESSIBLE AREAS OF THE PROPERTY IN CONJUNCTION WITH THAT INQUIRY, STATES THE FOLLOWING:
_____
_____

Agent (Broker
Representing Seller)_____ By_____ Date_____
                     (PLEASE PRINT)   (ASSOCIATE LICENSEE OR BROKER-SIGNATURE)

IV
AGENT'S INSPECTION DISCLOSURE
(To be completed only if the agent who has obtained the offer is other than the agent above.)
THE UNDERSIGNED, BASED ON A REASONABLY COMPETENT AND DILIGENT VISUAL INSPECTION OF THE ACCESSIBLE AREAS OF THE PROPERTY, STATES THE FOLLOWING:
_____
_____

Agent (Broker
obtaining the Offer)_____ By_____ Date_____
                     (PLEASE PRINT)   (ASSOCIATE LICENSEE OR BROKER-SIGNATURE)

V
BUYER(S) AND SELLER(S) MAY WISH TO OBTAIN PROFESSIONAL ADVICE AND/OR INSPECTIONS OF THE PROPERTY AND TO PROVIDE FOR APPROPRIATE PROVISIONS IN A CONTRACT BETWEEN BUYER AND SELLER(S) WITH RESPECT TO ANY ADVICE/INSPECTIONS/DEFECTS.

I/WE ACKNOWLEDGE RECEIPT OF A COPY OF THIS STATEMENT.

Seller_____ Date_____ Buyer_____ Date_____

Seller_____ Date_____ Buyer_____ Date_____

Agent (Broker
Representing Seller)_____ By_____ Date_____
                     (PLEASE PRINT)   (ASSOCIATE LICENSEE OR BROKER-SIGNATURE)

Agent (Broker
obtaining the Offer)_____ By_____ Date_____
                     (PLEASE PRINT)   (ASSOCIATE LICENSEE OR BROKER-SIGNATURE)

A REAL ESTATE BROKER IS QUALIFIED TO ADVISE ON REAL ESTATE. IF YOU DESIRE LEGAL ADVICE, CONSULT YOUR ATTORNEY.

This form is available for use by the entire real estate industry. The use of this form is not intended to identify the user as a REALTOR®. REALTOR® is a registered collective membership mark which may be used only by real estate licensees who are members of the NATIONAL ASSOCIATION OF REALTORS® and who subscribe to its Code of Ethics.

Copyright© 1990, CALIFORNIA ASSOCIATION OF REALTORS®
525 South Virgil Avenue, Los Angeles, California 90020

BROKER'S COPY

Page 2 of _____ Pages.

OFFICE USE ONLY
Reviewed by Broker or Designee _____
Date _____

EQUAL HOUSING OPPORTUNITY
M-PM-5/94

REAL ESTATE TRANSFER DISCLOSURE STATEMENT (TDS-14 PAGE 2 OF 2)

The Value of Home Improvements

The Value of Home Improvements

Remodeling can make a house more valuable as well as more livable. Although the cash poured into improvements seldom yields a dollar-for-dollar return when the house is sold, some types of remodeling return more of the investment than others. Keep in mind, however, that no matter how much is invested in improvements, it's ultimately the marketplace that determines what the home is worth.

The following list shows the payback potential of 20 popular remodelings:

Remodeling Projects and How They Pay Off

Type of Improvement	Recovery Cost (percentage)
Room addition	70–90
Major kitchen remodeling	45–70
Minor kitchen remodeling	60–80
New bath	75–100
Bathroom remodeling	60–80
Master suite	60–80
Reroofing	10–30
Finished basement	30–45
Garage	30–50
Windows and doors	25–45
Insulation	0–25
New heating system	30–45
Deck	65–75
Sun space	5–20
Swimming pool	0–65+ (varies by market)
Skylight	0–30
Exterior painting	40–50
Siding	15–35
Landscaping	45–65
Energy-efficient fireplace	75–100

Competitive Market Analysis

Competitive Market Analysis

Date _____

Sugg. list price $ _____

Comparative Market Analysis for _____

Address	Style	Const	Age	No. of Rms	No. of Bdrms	No. of Baths	Gar	Fplc	Pool	C/A	Size Prop	Assess Value	Taxes	Comments & Extras				

1. SIMILAR HOMES RECENTLY SOLD: These tell us what people are willing to pay . . . for this kind of home . . . in this area . . . at this time.

Closed Price   Date   Adj. Price

Fair Market Value

2. SIMILAR HOMES FOR SALE NOW: These tell us what we are competing against. Buyers will compare your home against these homes.

Askg Price   Days on Mkt.

3. EXPIRED LISTINGS—SIMILAR HOMES UNSOLD FOR 90 DAYS OR MORE: These illustrate the problems of overpricing.

PROBLEMS OF OVERPRICING: A. HARD to get salespeople excited.   B. HARD to get people to make an offer.
C. HARD to get good buyers to look.   D. HARD to get financing.

SOURCE: John E. Cyr and Joan m. Sobeck, *Real Estate Brokerage: A Success Guide* (Chicago: Real Estate Education Company, 1992), p. 244.

Cutaway View of a Typical House with Areas to Check

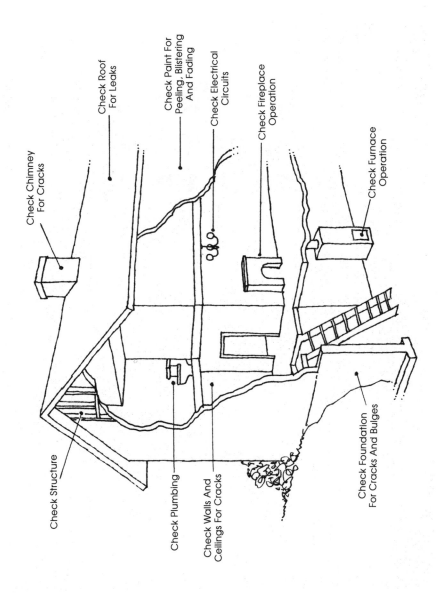

GLOSSARY

accrued Accumulated over a period of time, such as accrued interest or accrued expenses: accrued expenses, such as real estate taxes, have been incurred but are not yet payable; in a closing statement, accrued expenses are credited to the buyer, who will pay these expenses at a later date for the benefit of the seller

adjustable-rate mortgage (ARM) A loan whose interest rate is changed periodically to keep pace with current levels

agent A person authorized to work on behalf of another in dealing with third parties

amortization The schedule of periodic payments, usually monthly, made to a bank or other lender on a mortgage

appraisal An unbiased estimate of a property's value by a qualified professional

asking price The price at which a property is offered by the seller or broker

assumable mortgage A loan that may be passed to the next owner of the property

basis A home's value for tax purposes

broker A person licensed to represent homebuyers or homesellers for a fee or commission

buydown The payment of additional points to a mortgage lender in return for a lower interest rate on the loan

buyer's agent An agent who works for the best interests of the buyer, not the seller

buyers' market A market in which the supply of homes for sale exceeds demand

capital gain Taxable profit earned from the sale of an appreciated asset

caveat emptor A Latin phrase meaning "let the buyer beware"

closing The meeting at which the seller gives title to the buyer in exchange for the agreed-upon purchase price; also called a **settlement**

closing costs Expenses in addition to the purchase price of the property that must be paid by the buyer or deducted from the proceeds of the sale to the seller at the time of closing

closing statement A detailed cash accounting of a real estate sale, showing all cash received, all charges and credits made and all cash paid out in the transaction; also called a **settlement statement**

commission Payment to a broker for services rendered, such as in the sale or purchase of a home; usually a percentage of the selling price of the property

comparables Properties used in an appraisal report or competitive market analysis that are substantially equivalent to the subject property

competitive market analysis (CMA) A method of estimating the current market value of a listing seller's home by comparing the prices of recently sold homes that are similar in location, style and amenities

contingency Condition included as part of a sales contract that must be satisfied before the contract becomes binding

conventional mortgage A loan that is not FHA-insured or guaranteed by the VA; the most common home financing method

counteroffer An offer made by the buyer or seller in response to the other's offer

curb appeal Term for everything prospective buyers can see from the street that might want them to take a closer look at a house for sale

deed A formal document that transfers title from the seller to the buyer

default A failure to perform according to the terms of a contract

documentary tax stamp See **transfer tax**

down payment That part of the purchase price paid from a buyer's own funds, as opposed to the part that is financed

dual agent An agent who, with the informed written consent of buyer and seller, acts on behalf of both parties; may not represent the interests of one party to the exclusion or detriment of the other; and may not disclose one party's negotiating strategy or motivations to the other

earnest money A deposit made by a buyer when he or she makes an offer on a house; forfeited if the buyer defaults, but applied to the purchase price if the sale is closed

equity The difference in dollars between how much a house is worth and how much you owe on it

escrow Money or documents held by a third party until all terms of a contract are met

escrow account A bank account maintained by a real estate broker for holding money, such as a buyer's earnest money and the seller's taxes and insurance payment

exclusive agency A listing agreement in which sellers owe no commission if they find a buyer for their house on their own

exclusive right-to-sell A listing agreement in which sellers owe commission even if they find a buyer for their house on their own

fair market value See **market value**

FHA loans Mortgage loans made by banks and other lenders, but insured by the Federal Housing Administration

fixed-rate mortgage A loan that has an unchanging interest rate over its term

fixture An item of personal property that has become permanently attached to the real estate; is sold automatically with a house unless specifically excluded from the sale

HUD Department of Housing and Urban Development

improvements Permanent additions that increase the value of a house

inspection clause Provision in a sales contract that makes the contract contingent on the findings of a professional home inspector

interest Money paid to a lender as compensation for money that is borrowed

listing agreement A written contract in which the homeowner agrees to pay a commission to the real estate broker who finds a buyer who can meet the specified terms

listing presentation Proposal submitted by a real estate agent who seeks to put a prospective seller's property on the market

loan origination fee A charge incurred by a borrower to cover the administrative costs of the lender in making a loan; typically stated as a percentage of the loan

market value The most probable price real estate should bring in a sale occurring under normal market conditions

mortgage A lien or claim that a lender receives on a property as security for the loan it makes to a homebuyer

Multiple Listing Service (MLS) Arrangement by which brokers work together on the sale of each other's listed homes, with shared commissions

net listing Arrangement under which the seller receives a specified amount from the sales price and the broker keeps the rest as commission; illegal in many states

overimprovement Permanent addition or improvement in which the cost is greater than the increased value of the house

PITI Acronym for principal, interest, taxes and insurance—the four parts of an all-inclusive monthly mortgage payment

PMI Acronym for private mortgage insurance, required by many lenders when a borrower's down payment is less than 20 percent of the purchase price; protects the lender by paying off the loan should the borrower default

points The amount lending institutions charge in exchange for lowering the interest rate; one point equals one percent of the mortgage loan amount

prequalifying The lender's process of determining whether a borrower is creditworthy and capable of making payments on a loan

principal The amount of money borrowed

prorations Expenses (taxes, interest, insurance and other costs) divided between buyer and seller at closing

purchase-money mortgage A loan given by the seller to the buyer to cover part of the sales price; normally used to fill the gap between the buyer's down payment and the mortgage (Example: A buyer pays 10 percent in cash, gets an 80 percent first mortgage from a bank, and then the seller takes back a purchase-money second mortgage for the remaining 10 percent)

REALTOR® Registered name for a member of the National Association of REALTORS®

sales comparison approach The process of estimating the value of property through examination and comparison of actual sales of comparable properties

sales contract A document that sets forth all details of the agreement between a buyer and a seller for the sale and purchase of a house. Also known as an **offer to purchase,** a **contract of purchase and sale** and a **purchase agreement**

seller's agent A real estate licensee who is employed by and acts as the agent of the seller only, with fiduciary duties of loyalty, confidentiality and obedience to the seller; and honesty, fairness and full disclosure of known facts materially affecting the property's condition to both the buyer and the seller

sellers' market Market in which the demand for homes exceeds the supply for sale

settlement See **closing**

term The length of time in which a loan is to be paid off

title The right of property ownership

title insurance Policy that protects the lender and buyer against loss or damage due to defects in the title of a property

title search The process of checking public records to make sure that no adverse claims affect the value of the title

transfer tax Tax stamps required to be affixed to a deed by state and/or local law

VA loan Mortgage loans guaranteed by the Department of Veterans Affairs (VA) and made available through banks and other lending institutions; reserved for active military personnel and veterans

walk-through inspection Final inspection of a property's condition by the buyer, to make sure all conditions in the sales contract have been met

INDEX

ABOUT THE AUTHOR

Over the past 25 years, the CENTURY 21® name has held the distinction of being the undisputed leader in the real estate industry. We have helped millions of people through the exciting adventure of selling their home or finding the home of their dreams. In the relocation process as well, CENTURY 21® experts have been with families every step of the way.

To meet the high expectations of today's demanding, value-conscious consumer, the CENTURY 21® System now offers an array of home-related products and services, including CENTURY 21® Home Improvements^{SM}, computer online listings and homebuyer information services, *CENTURY 21® House & Home* magazine and other housing-related services.

As America enters the 21st century, the nation's best-trained home ownership experts are at your service at each and every one of the CENTURY 21® System's 6,000 independently owned offices in all 50 states and throughout the world.